T0104413

Cottleville:
Where History Never Grows Old

A Cottle Family Story

Second Edition

Cottleville:
Where History Never Grows Old
A Cottle Family Story

Second Edition

By Sheryl Kay Guffey

Cottle Grist Mill and Creek
South Woodstock, VT (2011).

Order this book online at www.trafford.com
or email orders@trafford.com

Most Trafford titles are also available at major online book retailers.

© Copyright 2017 Sheryl Kay Guffey.
All rights reserved. No part of this publication may be reproduced, stored in a
retrieval system, or transmitted, in any form or by any means, electronic, mechanical,
photocopying, recording, or otherwise, without the written prior permission of the author.

Print information available on the last page.

ISBN: 978-1-4907-7730-6 (sc)
ISBN: 978-1-4907-7731-3 (hc)
ISBN: 978-1-4907-7732-0 (e)

Library of Congress Control Number: 2016915556

Because of the dynamic nature of the Internet, any web addresses or links contained in
this book may have changed since publication and may no longer be valid. The views
expressed in this work are solely those of the author and do not necessarily reflect the
views of the publisher, and the publisher hereby disclaims any responsibility for them.

Any people depicted in stock imagery provided by Thinkstock are models,
and such images are being used for illustrative purposes only.
Certain stock imagery © Thinkstock.

Trafford rev. 06/27/2017

Trafford
PUBLISHING® www.trafford.com

North America & international
toll-free: 1 888 232 4444 (USA & Canada)
fax: 812 355 4082

DEDICATION

This book is dedicated to all the pioneering spirits of yesteryear and today. Without our enthusiasts and stargazers who put their energy and spirit into the development of this region, it very well may remain the muddy lowland the first Western explorers found. Pride and independence has always been a theme, change and preservation has always been a chapter.

Second Edition. Many thanks to all the wonderful people of Cottleville, who assisted in the preparation of this book. *Cottleville: Where History Never Grows Old, A Cottle Family Story.* The town meetings, the shared documents and pictures and the encouragement to write it all down, comes from many fine individuals who share the passion to tell this region's history. These include: St. Charles County Executive Steve Ehlmann, Joseph L. Harl, Past Mayor Don Yarber, Past Mayor Steve Kochanski, Mayor Jim Hennessey, City Administrator Rich Francis, St. Charles County Sheriff Scott Lewis, Retired Fire Chief Rob Wylie, Cottleville Community Fire Protection District, Captain Assistant Chief of Professional Services Bob and Dawn Church, Karen Conley, David and Dorothy Kappeller, Judith Kuhl, Ruth Lauer, Frank Martin, Mike Reiter, Clarence and Marleen Schlueter (Wilcox), Dolores Voelmer, and, many others. I truly appreciate the assistance from the St. Charles County Historical Society and it's staff. A special thanks, goes to my family, especially: Alva Spellman, Dennis C. Spellmann and Carol Sue Spellmann, Dr. Ryan Vance Guffey, Daniel Dennis Guffey

Andrew Cottle, James Schwabe, Velma Cottle Musick, and John, Jan, and Ben Friberg, who kept the love of history in their hearts and took the time to save, update, and make available their genealogical records.

A beautiful landscape of property in Cottleville overlooking the Dardenne bottom land owned by the late Dennis C. Spellmann.
Picture by Sheryl Guffey (2010)

PREFACE

"Far and away the best prize that life offers is the chance to work hard at work worth doing." Teddy Roosevelt

The preparation of this book has been my chance to "work hard at work worth doing" and has become a true love and passion. My intent is to provide others with the opportunity to embrace Cottleville's storied past and enjoy the heritage it has to offer. I also write this book with the aspiration that we should celebrate the historic renovations of our city with pride and appreciation. Within our shared collective memory, we keep what is best as treasure forever. Indian tribes, Spanish conquistadors, French expansionists, European migrants, Revolutionary War Heroes and American frontiersman began the journey of exploration in the area known as Cottleville, which was founded in 1839 by Lorenzo Cottle, and all have called it home.

The forward thinking vision of the future, which is intrinsically tied to the past, demonstrates the pride in and longevity of our fabled city, Cottleville. Many have found it to be a refuge from the hectic world, with a quaint and magical feel. Cottleville is a special place where all can embrace its uniqueness with love and awe, pride and dreams.

In 2003, Cottleville celebrated its 150th anniversary. In 2009, the City of Cottleville passed legislation to revitalize the "downtown" area with wider sidewalks that are stamped concrete to look like the Old Western Plank road timbers. There are also inlaid brick pedestrian walkways and historic lighting, all designed to provide a "feel" and "look" of the early 1900s. In 2011, Cottleville began this historic transformation toward revitalization. The past reaches up to all who want to continue and participate in its heritage. Let's begin our journey.

Amesbury Massa

Table of Contents

Chapter 1

Geography and Its Impact

Cottleville is situated near the basins of three great rivers: the Ohio, the Missouri, and the Mississippi. The geological setting of Cottleville was in the Glacial Plains, which, during the ice age, is where giant glaciers deposited crushed and ground rock called drift. Wind carried fine rock and pulverized soil that blanketed the area. This process transformed the land and initiated the environmental and agricultural conditions we see today. However, Cottleville is now located in what geologists call the Middle Dardenne Basin, which is only 495 feet above sea level and has a land mass of 4.5 square miles.

Cottleville is one of the oldest towns in St. Charles County, located about 10 miles west of St. Charles and the Mississippi River, butting up to the Dardenne waterway. Indian trails turned into roads leading westward through Missouri for covered wagons and stage and mail coaches. Situated about a day's journey from the Mighty Mississippi, many early travelers would find themselves stranded when the Dardenne River — now Dardenne Creek — would overflow.

Location of Cottleville, Missouri
Coordinates: 38°45'7"N 90°39'12"W

Cottleville encompasses about 100 acres that stretch from Dardenne Creek as the northern perimeter, the Crooked Creek as the western perimeter, Gutermuth Road as the southern perimeter, and Mid Rivers Mall Dr. as the eastern perimeter. The reason settlers in the 16th century chose this specific territorial layout was due to the vast amount of available natural resources. Crooked Creek and Dardenne River (Creek) frequently over ran its boundaries, laying down fertile silt for its neighbors.

"Cottleville lies within a virtual 'Garden of Eden'. This contributed to the growth and variety of prairies, oak and hickory forest, and river ecosystems each having distinctive flora and fauna that are easily accessible and provided a wide range of foods from which to select. The rich fertile soils that were widely available made farming a very productive enterprise for prehistoric and historic inhabitants alike. This region also contained the resources needed for organic medicines, wood construction and eventually manufacturing. Wildlife was very abundant and continues to be home to many deer, turkey, geese, ducks and birds." 1.

Many years ago, a variety of cultures inhabited Missouri, which was also known as the area with "those who have dugout canoes" or the "settlement of the big canoes" or even "Big Muddy." To date, the earliest residents that came to inhabit the Cottleville region did so approximately 8000 B.C. At that time, the landscape was considerably different from what we see today. The climate was more humid and rarely reached even 80 degrees. The flood plains near the rivers were strikingly fertile as a result of the frequent shifting of the water passages. "Forest composition on the floodplain was affected by two factors. One was the frequency and duration of flooding, and the other was the type of plant succession on land being built up by sedimentation" 1. As a result, this became a prime location for the first inhabitants to establish a community.

Many archeological projects have been performed within the last 40 years by Dan Haas and Roger Boyd. Archeological excavations have uncovered mollusks in backwater areas and streams. These hard shelled mollusks appear to not only have been used as a source of food, but as tools. The shells could be ground and used as binding agents for ceramic vessels, carved into jewelry, or used as digging instruments. The number of total recorded sites within St. Charles County is over a thousand and Cottleville had its share of cultures.

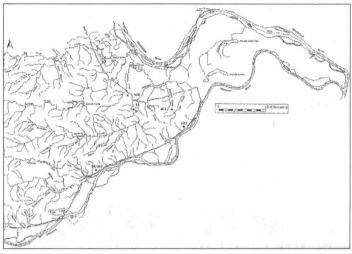

**Early Archaic Period
Location of Dalton Sites in St. Charles County
(8000–7000 B.C.)**

A camp 100 by 50 meters on a bluff top near the Dardenne Creek, reveals projectile points. 2.

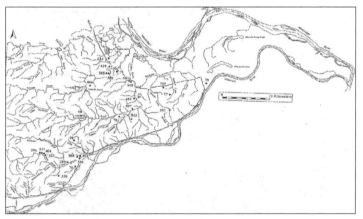

**Location of Middle Archaic Sites in St. Charles County
(5000–3000 B.C.)**

Camps found on the Dardenne Creek within this period measure: 50 by 20 meters, 180 by 160 meters, 320 x 200 meters, and 120 by 80 meters. 3

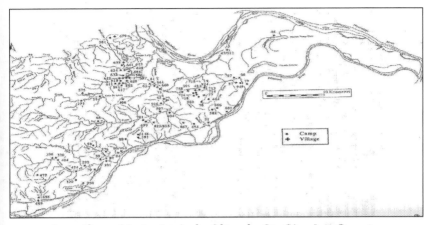

Location of Late Archaic Sites in St. Charles County (3000–500 B.C.) 4.

Many other projects for archeological data have been performed in the St. Charles County area, resulting in a total of 82 reported sites from the Late Archaic Period. The Cottleville area has five of these sites documented on the Dardenne and Crooked Creeks as villages, campsites and lithic scatters.

FIGURE 43: Location of Potential Redistribution Centers.
Identified by Harl, Wright, and Nixon (1986:156, Map 10)

Location of Potential Redistribution Centers of Middle Woodland Period (2,500 B.C.–1,600 B.C.)

These sites were identified by Joseph Harl, Patti Wright and Joseph Nixon in 1986. 5.

An article in the *St. Louis Post-Dispatch*, August 12, 1966, entitled "Traces of Early Indian Village are Found in St. Charles County," told of the Late Woodland Indian presence in Cottleville. The article describes 17 dark spots in the back yard of Ambrose Schulte, native of Cottleville, which when unearthed proved to be storage and refuse holes dating to about 1000 A.D. Schulte stated, "I had knocked a couple of feet of dirt off of a knoll behind a home we're building. I noticed some arrow heads, but didn't pay any mind because they're quite common in this part of the country."

Schulte owned a 35-acre site on Gutermuth Road, which is within eye sight of Cottleville. It was soon discovered that two round houses and a rectangular house had been there and that they were part of a village dating to slightly before the culture that built Cahokia Mounds. Legend has it that an ancient Indian cemetery exists near Schulte's property. Arrow points, as well as three point and four point arrow heads were found at the site. My father, Dennis Spellmann—a Cottle descendant—owned property near the Schulte farm and we could also find arrowheads every spring when the land was tilled to put in a large garden.

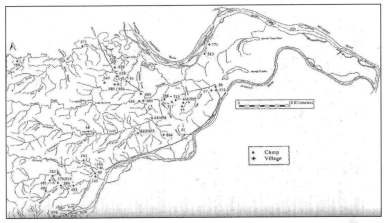

Location of Late Woodland Sites in St. Charles County (1,600-1,000 A.D.) 6.

"Looking to Preserve History," an article in the *St. Charles Post-Dispatch* dated November 29, 1988, describes the story of Gerald and Georgette Bergen. Their three-story house was built in the 1890s by a physician who used the side building as the Cottleville doctor's office. Both the Doctor's office and the 1870 home still stand in the historic district. The Bergens restored the home and spent hours digging for artifacts with great success.

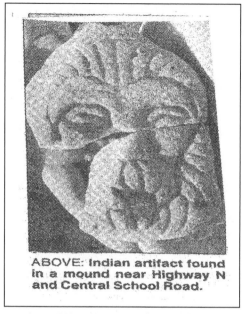

ABOVE: Indian artifact found in a mound near Highway N and Central School Road.

Late Woodland Indian Artifact

Some of the first Indian tribes known to have resided in Missouri were the Missouris, Dakotas, Iowas, Osages, and Poncas. "The Missouris was the chief tribe in the area of Cottleville with villages as large as 150 to 300 acres, but were finally absorbed in to other tribes. It is estimated that there were 300,000 Indians when the white man came." *St. Charles Missouri Bicentennial Historical Program Book 1769-1969.* Stephen Kochanski, then chairman of the Cottleville Trustees, was quoted as saying, "We know we can't stop progress but we want to try to save the historic part of the village." *St. Charles Post- Dispatch,* November 29, 1988. The appreciation of Indian cultures and history became paramount to many Cottleville residents.

Indian Trail Marking Tree in Cottleville. Picture by City of Cottleville (2009).

Indians bent this tree, located within Cottleville Legacy Park, as a sapling to mark a specific direction to a specific object, such as a creek, food, trail, or another trail tree.

What goes without saying is that archaeological investigations allow us to document this rich heritage and provide us with a better understanding of the amazing accomplishments the past inhabitants had achieved. This is reinforced by Ralph Waldo Emerson, who suggested that the confluence of the Missouri River with the Mississippi made the area "the greatest cross-roads the world ever saw." 7

The first European explorers of the Cottleville area were of Spanish descent. They came in 1541 under the direction of Hernando de Soto. The first French explorers, Father Jacques Marquette and Louis Joliet came from Canada in 1673 and set foot on land that would later become Missouri. In 1682, Rene-Robert Cavelier, sieur de La Salle took possession of the whole Mississippi valley in the name of King Louis XIV of France and named it Louisiana. The secret Treaty of Fontainebleau in November of 1762, ceded French territory west of the Mississippi River to Spain. Three months later, in February of 1763, the Treaty of Paris allowed the Spanish to formally obtain the Louisiana Territory from France. The first Spanish grant of "common fields" was made in 1790. France regained Louisiana from Spain under the secret Treaty of San Ildefonso in 1800.

Carlos Cardinal settled along the Dardenne River in 1789, which later became the settlement of St. Peters. Cottleville at that time was called Pin Hook, perhaps because the directionality of the creeks resembled the shape of a pin hook. Cottleville was also known as the Dardenne Township. The name Dardenne comes from Toussaint Dardenne family. Dardenne, a French trapper, bought a house along the creek that would bear his name in August of 1750. John Coontz began operating a water mill in 1790, mainly for French settlers. Coontz was a German who lived in Illinois before moving to the Dardenne Valley. Another early pioneer on the Dardenne was Jean Baptiste Blandeau, who arrived in 1796. Warren Cottle led a 40-family migration of 100 people to Dardenne in 1799. In 1803, the Louisiana Purchase transferred land to the possession of the United States. Cottleville has been under three flags as well as a center of conflict through the Civil War.

Chapter 2

The Cottle Migration

It goes without saying that a book about Cottleville could not be made without a lengthy review of the Cottle founders and their descendents. Many families of Cottleville can walk the trail with the Cottles through their own lineage and adventurous stories. The past can touch each of us as we explore how these migrations occurred.

The family surname, Cottle, has persisted for centuries, appearing first in the time of the Roman Empire in the Latin form, Cotta. There are traces of the same root word prior to the Roman period. It is possible that the name was in existence in Egypt during the time of that great civilization, since it has been found in Egyptian carving.

Accuracy in tracing the name begins with the French Norman period of European history. In the French form the name is COUTELLE. A branch of the family migrating to Germany during the time of Charlemagne set up the name variation Cottschalk, which is simply the Germanic form of the present name COTTLE. With the Norman conquest of England, the French Knights of this name went to England. They were a virile and adventurous people, eager for wealth and power gained by the incasion under William the Conqueror. Seen after 1100 the name is recorded in England in the Anglo-French form COTTELL. John di Cothuelle, born in 1277, is an example of the middle English language period which used the suffix le. At this time in England we find the name of Roger Cotel listed on the Hundred Rolls, or tax books. The modern English language with its fixed forms of spelling was established. The variations of this name as they appear in England of that time are all vouched for as the field of proper names. The modern Doomsday Book of England carries reference to Cottle as being of the old middle English language period using Cothuelle or Cotel.

In England the early seat of the Cottle family was at Atworth, Wiltshire, near Melkham in England. On November 8, 1580, the family was admitted into the nobility of England by Queen Elizabeth I, who recognized North Taunton Cottle and possibly his brother, Samford Peverel Cottle. This coat of arms is still found in a mural on the wall of the church in Bradford-on-Avon. This coat of arms was displayed in several parishes, churches, and manor houses in Wiltshire, Somerset, and Devonshire. The Cottle coat of arms is stated by Aubrey Hoare in his "History of Wilts" 8., and by other historians to have been a shield of gold with a bend (diagonal band from the upper right to the lower left) of red and on the ducal crown a tiger sejant.

The Coat of Arms of the Cottle Family

"The first Cottle of record to come to America was William Cottle (1626-1660), who was brought here on *"The Confidence of London"* in April, 1638. He is listed as one of four servants of a John Sanders of "Lanford" Landford, Wiltshire, England."9. It was not uncommon for young men to be brought to America as servants or apprentices. William was only 12 years old when he arrived. After becoming of age and completing his term of service, William Cottle established himself at Salisbury near the mouth of the Merrimac River, in the colony of Massachusetts Bay and then in Newbury. William died at the age of 34 in Newbury Mass. The City of Cottleville can trace it's lineage from **Edward Cottle, Jr** (1628-1710), William's brother, Edward was two years younger than William. (Note: Boldfaced names in the text are bloodline relatives.)

Edward Cottle married Judith Osgood on his 21st birthday, 1650, in his hometown of Wiltshire, England, and announced their intentions to sail to the American colonies to make their home. He joined William Cottle Massachusetts in 1651. Edward then founded and lived in Amesbury (Salisbury New Town), Mannamoiett of Cape Cod, Nantucket Island, see page viii and Tisbury-Martha's Vineyard. Edward died on June 1710 at another town he founded—Chilmark, Massachusetts—at the age of 82.

Children of Edward, Jr and Judith Cottle (Osgood):

Edward, II b. January 17, 1652; d. April 15, 1653

Mary, b. November 1, 1653; m. Samuel Bickford d. May 21, 1706

Benjamin, b. March 2, 1655; d. 1710

Sarah, b. March, 1656; d. 1659

Judith, b. March 5, 1659; d. young

Hannah, b. ca. 1661; m. John Hillman d. 1728

Elizabeth, b. April 19, 1663; bound out to Thomas Barnett d. 1670

Edward, b. September 28, 1666 d. November 1751; m. Esther (Daggett) (half-breed Indian, daughter of Joseph Daggett by his Indian wife, Alice Sissston, daughter of the Sachem of Sanehacantacket, an American Indian Princess); m. Abigail (Allen), b.1663; d. December 25, 1733

Ezra (son) 1662 May 5 - 1749 Oct 30

James, b. ca.1668; m. Elizabeth (Look) November 1675, d. 1750

Judith, b. April 13, 1670; no further record

Lydia, b. May 17, 1672; no further record

Ann, b. March 3, 1673 d. 1737; m. Isaac Robinson

John, b. September 7, 1675 d. October 1705; m. **Jane (Look)** 1700- b. December 24, 1680 d. 1756

Samuel, b. 1676; d. in 1698

Dorothy 1678-1681, Oct 1.

John Cottle bought 20 acres of land from his father, which included a mill; married Jane Look in 1700; and built a home near his father's house in Tisbury-Martha's Vineyard. Three children were born to the young couple in 1702,1704 and 1706; however, in 1705, John died leaving his pregnant wife to care for the family. Two of Edward's children eventually ran the mill: Sylvanus and John.

> The Cottle boys, they ran a mill;
> sometimes it went, sometimes stood still;
> And when it went, it made no noise;
> Because' twas run by the Cottle boys.
> "An old jingle"

Children of John Cottle and Jane Cottle (Look)

Lydia, b. September 14, 1702 – d. December 30, 1725
Sylvanus, b. May 9, 1704 – d. December 9, 1785 m.
 Martha (Hatch) Dec. 9, 1725 b. 1708 d. 1741, m.
 Abigail (Sherman) February 18, 1745 daughter of
 Major William Bradford of the Mayflower
John, b. April 10, 1706 – d. February 1804 m. Zerviah
 Hillman 1731

Sylvanus was only 17 months old when his father died and was adopted by his aunt, Anne Cottle Robinson. Sylvanus had 13 children, eight by **Martha (Hatch)** and five by **Abigail (Sherman)**, whom he married in 1745. Abigail, a granddaughter of **Governor William Bradford** (listed as being on the Mayflower in 1620), was born in Rochester, Massachusetts, on July 27, 1721, and was the twin of John Sherman. Sylvanus became an antipedobaptist, which did not allow for baptism of infants. Sylvanus and Abigail's children had baptismal records before the birth of Warren Cottle, but none after.

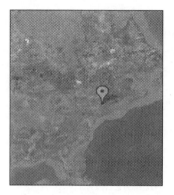

In 1760, Sylvanus moved his family and second wife from Martha's Vineyard to Rochester, New York. Abigail Sherman Cottle was from the congested Rochester area and sought more land for all of the children. The Cottle family signed what they believed to be valid land contracts, and prepared to move to the frontier. A total of 318 families constituted the original settlers in the area, but a decade of protests and injunction by King George III kept the actual population small. This changed when Vermont was officially recognized as a territory, separate from New York, in 1790. There was a great exodus from Martha's Vineyard that was contemporary to the time that Sylvanus, Abigail and Warren left the Vineyard in the 1760s.

> "The sandy soil was a major factor in the island's economy for, almost without exception, the settlers were English yeomen and farmers. The soil of the Vineyard was best adapted to sheep raising-an industry which required such large acreage that it was not long before the need for more farmland was acute, a second powerful factor in family emigrations." 10

Meanwhile, the Treaty of Fontainebleau ceded territory west of the Mississippi River from France to Spain in 1762. In 1771, town records show that Sylvanus

Cottle served in Joseph Marsh's Regiment of Militia. Town records also state that the brothers Sylvanus and Joseph Cottle went to Woodstock, Vermont (still within the boundaries of New York) in 1772 to explore the area. Sylvanus and Joseph moved to Woodstock and selected land for their extended family.

Children of Sylvanus and Martha (Hatch) Cottle b. 1708 d. 1741 m. December 9, 1725:

Issac, b. September 7, 1726 d. before 1769 m. Mary (Clark)

Edward, b. July 25, 1728

Benjamin, b. March 17, 1729 d. about 1762 m. Sarah (Smith)

Ann, b. June 6, 1732 d. November 25, 1815 m. Simon Athearn ca. 1750 d. 1808

Lydia, b. August 22, 1733 m. William Weeks

Jane, b. February 11, 1736 no further record

Kesiah, b. October 25, 1737; m. Cornelius Norton d. 1783

Mary, b. June 7, 1741; m. James Cowing October 29, 1763 d. Dec. 31, 1780

Children of Sylvanus and Abigail Cottle (Sherman) b. July 27, 1721 d. after 1773 m. February 18, 1745:

Jabez b. February 22 1747 d. June 4, 1820 m. Sarah (Arnold) d. June 28, 1829—struck by lighting

Sylvanus Jr., b. June 15 1750 d. December 1811 m. Louisa (Power), reported to have been the first wedding in Woodstock (Missouri land grant 500 arpents in 1804) An arpent was a French unit of land measurement, equivalent to 0.84 acres. Thus, 500 arpents equals 420 acres.)

Joseph. (Deacon), b. July 28 1753 d. 1854: m. Azubah (Power) 1775. Daughter **Minerva Cottle** m. Zaddock Woods 1795 b. 1755 d.1830.

Warren, b.1755 d. April 11, 1811; m. Relief (Farnsworth) June 28, 1781 b. November 17, 1762, d. June 1, 1842

John, b. 1757 d.1825; m. **Elizabeth** (Allen) (**Warren Jr.,** m. their daughter **Salome**)

Martha, m. Jonathan Farnsworth b. July 28, 1759

Warren Cottle was born in Cape Cod, Mass. and then lived in New York. He was 18 years old when he moved from New York to Vermont. He married **Relief (Farnsworth)** in 1761, and they had five boys and two girls. Warren and his brother Jabez did not settle in Cottle Town, but bought land nearby that later became the village of South Woodstock. In his monumental book, *History of Woodstock*, Henry Swan Dana, the town's longest serving Town Clerk, wrote in 1888 that it was generally considered that the Cottle family was the first people to settle in what is now the village of South Woodstock. 13.

Warren became known as "Capt." Warren Cottle for his military service in the Revolutionary War. 1775-1783

"Joseph and Sylvanus Jr. Cottle of Martha's Vineyard were the first of this family to come to our town. They were in the South Parish. Jabez and Warren followed the first ones: they were energetic, enterprising men. While owning farms, they built mills and started stores. They took an active part in the early town meetings and held all sorts of offices. Sylvanus and Joseph settled in the Fletcher region and the Cottles so multiplied there, that it was called Cottletown." 11.

"The forty children of their five sons helped generate a Cottle population that would grow so large the area came to be known locally as "Cottle Town." 12

Children of Captain Warren and Relief Cottle (Farnsworth)

Marshall, b. 1779 d. Sept 4 1801 at age 22; m. Hannah (Bailey) September 11, 1800 by Jabez Cottle - her uncle

Ira (Muxey) b.1780 d.1842 Lincoln Co.; m. Susan (Suby) Cottle, cousin

Dr. Warren Jr., b.1781 d. June 1823 m. **Salome Cottle**, (cousin) 1801

Oliver, b.1783 d.1827 of yellow fever in New Orleans m. Charity (Lowe) of Tennessee, 1808

Stephen, b. 1784 d. 1829 in Texas, m. Sally (Turner) November 10, 1808 Lincoln Co.

Letitia, b. 1785 d. 1799 in Missouri

When Vermont entered the Union as the 14th state in 1791, 47 families moved into the Kedron Valley, increasing the need for mills and stores. Captain Warren Cottle opened a general store in 1793 and a second store in 1794 to expand on the first. New families were arriving in town every month, and with them came the basic needs of every frontier settlement. Citizens of South Woodstock shopped there regularly.

Cottle Gristmill and Store South Woodstock, Vermont

A miller ground whatever grain was brought to him, and charged a portion of the final product. The term "gristmill" describes a small mill open to all comers. Grist is grain that has been separated from its chaff in preparation of grinding. Maize (corn) made into grist is called grits when it is coarse and corn meal when it is finely ground. Wheat, oats, barley, and buckwheat are also ground and sifted into flour and farina. The proverb "all is grist for the mill" means "everything can be made useful, or be a source of profit."

Warren Cottle was the first Captain of the military company in the South Village. Captain Cottle trained as a Minuteman in 1776, and served with the New Hampshire Regiment against British General John Burgoyne in 1777. Cottle led a company of Vermont militia later in the Revolutionary War. He served in the Late Alarm Vermont Militia in 1780 and 1781.14 Captain Cottle was elected as one of two men appointed to represent South Woodstock in the State Legislature as Representative to the General Assembly from the town of Woodstock, in the years 1780, 1781, and 1789.

Captain Warren Cottle was very active in the town's social, civic, and military life. In 1783, the U.S. and Great Britain had signed the final peace treaty in Paris ending the American Revolution. The next year, he was a constable, an overseer of highways, a grand juror, and an organizer of state government. Warren was the first trader in South Woodstock and started merchandising out of his home and then built a separate store. Captain Cottle did very well through these years and in the "Grand List of 1787" and was valued at 29 pounds, the highest amount of any of the Cottles.

Captain Warren and Relief Cottle Home

Captain Warren Cottle completed building a home for his family, in 1796 in South Woodstock, which still stands today.

The original house is of masonry construction, and the basement sits on bedrock. On the lower level, there is a large living room, dining room, kitchen, pantry, bathroom, and three fireplaces. Upstairs, there are four bedrooms and two baths. The home was recently for sale for the amount of $1.7 million. The adventurous spirit must have been strong for the Captain to leave this home and explore the new frontier.

**Warren Cottle Courtyard
in South Woodstock Vermont Property**

The stone wall behind the Cottle home has a carving possibly symbolizing Captain Cottle's infantry involvement.

Economics worsened around 1790, and Warren Cottle tried in vain for three years to keep his general store financially afloat. Captain Cottle began to consider other alternatives, including leaving the Kedron Valley. In conversations with merchants and French trappers who would occasionally drift through the Woodstock area, Warren learned of land openings far to the west along the Mississippi River.

The Orleans Territory, owned by Spain, sounded like Paradise to the New Englander. There were 3000 settlers, mostly French Canadians, living along the Mississippi and Missouri Rivers outside of St. Louis at this time. Many people believed that the climate in upper Louisiana provided a specific cure for consumption (an archaic name for tuberculosis). Captain Cottle, with the support of his family, made his plans to leave for Orleans in the spring of 1798. Captain Cottle was 41 when the gristmill and store closed. In the Administrator's papers of Captain Warren Cottle's estate located at the St. Charles County Historical Society, there is a statement which shows that Warren appointed his brother Jabez on February 16, 1798, to honor all of his debts, and to collect debts due him. Jabez was seven years older than Warren.

Jabez Cottle Home in South Woodstock, Vermont

Along Hwy 106, you can still see the house built by Jabez Cottle in 1812, which is about 0.25 mile from the Warren Cottle home.

Note - Compare the house structure built by Warren and Jabez.

Captain Warren Cottle and one of his sons, Ira (age 18 and nicknamed Muxey), traveled from the Kedron Valley along the Appalachian Trail. They went south across Massachusetts, Connecticut, and New York by horseback. The Cottles headed west on Forbes Road through Pennsylvania to the Ohio River, where they booked passage to the Indiana Territory. They walked the Vincennes Trail to St. Louis, arriving in the summer of 1798. The St. Charles District of Orleans consisted of the country west of St. Louis and the Missouri River bottom lands, still populated mostly by bear, bison, and Indians. The two men spent the summer making notes and drawing crude maps of the areas they traversed. They visited the few white men they encountered there, as well as with St. Charles and St. Louis authorities. Warren built a temporary home on the bank of the Missouri River, then the outpost of civilization. Warren Cottle made three excursions into the wilderness in search of a likely home site. He decided to settle west of St. Charles after his exploratory trips about 10 miles beyond the Missouri. Warren was impressed with the beautiful countryside, the big trees, the game, and the birds. It was dangerous country, for Indians who roamed through this district were certain to dispute any person trespassing on this land. His settlement eventually became of the City of Cottleville, named and laid out by his grandson Lorenzo.

The art of letter writing has come and gone for many; however, reading Warren Cottle's inspirational words brings to mind the power of words and written communication. His letter excited many New Englanders to venture westward.

The Happy Ground

From foreign lands to you, my friend, I write
With satisfaction and heartfelt delight,
Hoping these lines, when they arrive to thee,
Will find you as well as I, when they left me.

To tell you all the states I've traveled through,
And all the novelties that rose to view,
Till I embarked and on the liquid flood
Some thousand miles upon her surface rode;
How death appeared in horrible array
And snatched a youthful passenger away,
Scare nineteen, springs their fragrance on him shed
When lo! He's plunged into a watery bed;
To tell you all that's passed before my eyes
Would swell my letter to a monstrous size.

Suffice it then, I've found the happy ground,
Where fishes, beauty, and delights abound,
Where all the year in sweet profusions roll
And glads the eye, or charms the soul.
Unnumbered flowers o'er wide prairies spread,
The varying beauties as the seasons roll.
Regale the sense and captivate the souls.
Here the industrious bee extracts the sweets
And sips the dews from every flower she meets.
With loads of wax, collected here with care,
They build their waxen cells in neighboring trees.
Here numerous deer, and bear, and elk resort,
And buffaloes, to crown the huntsman's sport,
Here's hens and turkeys, caught with greatest ease,
Fattening on acorns falling from the trees.
The streams abound with various kinds of fish,
These crown our feasts, and form a dainty dish.

To quench the thirst and please the appetite,
Here's beaver, coon, and fox, to crown our heads,
While geese and swans, and ducks will fill our beds.

The prest wheat, the joyful husband sees
Waving their yellow heads with every breeze.
The earth spontaneous yields the best of corn,
Revokes that sentence, "Men for Toil were born".
The husbandman must sow and plant tis true,
But after that he has nothing more to do.
Here there's finest flax and hemp; and cotton grows
With which our women fabricate our clothes.

Here's bars of iron drawn from richest ore,
And mines lead—an inexhaustible store.
Here's caves where every crude material's hid
From which the explosive nitrous powder's made.

To crown the whole, perfect without a fault,
The almighty gave us springs of liquid salt,
And lakes, whose bottoms richly coverer o'er
With salt congealed in endless store.
If wondrous scenes delight your wondering eyes
Look once again and see new wonders rise:
A plain extending far beyond our sight,
Which spread with salt; like snow of purest white,
Its briny rills that trickle from the plain
Are by the sun congealed to salt again.
Here springs of purest oil profusely rise,
Of medical and healing qualities,
These feed our lamps and give a friendly light
When Sol retires and gives the reins to night.

Now with a living, kind, and faithful friend
In sweet discourse, the evening hours I'll spend.

The choicest fruits, the acid and the sweet,
Should grace my board and form a rural treat.
For here with boughs with yellow fruitage bend
With every breeze the mellowing fruits descend.
My friend and I in high discourse write,
On Eden while our parents were upright,
How modest Eve, in innocency drest,
Stood forth to entertain her angel guest,
How the great visitant accepts the treat
From the raised turf not scorns the mossy seat.
Behold the board, with choicest fruitage crowned
And nectarous draughts alternate passing round,
How Adam's heart dilates with gratitude
While Raphael, his greatest narrative pursued.
How heaven has here dispensed her bounties free,
No prohibition, no forbidden tree.

O'er ravished souls with retrospective view,
We count the wonders we have written you.
Here I would live, retired from noise and strife,
And spend delighted the remains of life.
Lulled by the nightingale at the close of day
Walked by the early robins sprightly lay,
Content and happy, till the time shall come
That God, my Father, sends and calls me home.
Warren Cottle 1800

This letter no doubt encouraged others to leave Vermont for the "Happy Ground," which lay in Missouri. Warren Cottle wrote this magnificent letter in April of 1800 from Dardenne, Louisiana Territory, (now Cottleville-St. Charles County, Missouri), to James Cowing in Woodstock, Vermont. "The original letter was in the possession of, Miss Janet McKay Cowing, now deceased, who was the granddaughter of James Cowing, Warren

Cottle's brother-in-law by marriage of his sister, Mary Cottle."15

Captain Warren Cottle left Ira to stay in the St. Charles District and returned to Vermont that fall of 1799, determined to make the move. By the time he arrived back to South Woodstock, their excitement had reached the contagious stage. Captain Cottle gathered his family at the inn and told of the beautiful lands they had seen and explained how inexpensive the tracts of land were, and of the accommodating spirit of the Spanish. A series of town meetings were called and many of the Woodstock citizens considered the possibility of moving west with Warren Cottle.

Captain Warren Cottle started on his final journey to Missouri in the fall of 1799 with the remainder of his family: brother Joseph, 46 yrs old and wife Azubah 44 yrs old; (Power) wife Relief 37; his oldest son, Marshall 20, who had just married Hannah, sister to Col. David Bailey, the first sheriff of Lincoln County; his sons, Dr. Warren, Oliver, Stephen; and his daughter, Letitia. Also making the trip were Sylvanus, Isaac Cottle, William Farnsworth, Johnathan and Keziah Woods (Keith), Sarah Woods, James and Rachael Woods, Martin Woods, Zadock and Minerva Woods (Cottle), along with six-month-old baby Minerva; and possibly Benjamin and Sarah Allen (Woods).

There was a large company of other settlers which Captain Cottle led from Vermont to the new land. A total of 40 families had agreed to be part of the westbound caravan. Including the children, there were exactly 100 persons that started from South Village (South Woodstock) for the west; some of the emigrants going as far as St. Charles District, Upper Louisiana (now Missouri). The journey at the turn of the 19th century was not for the faint in spirit, for all of this took place before the Louisiana Purchase and the pacification of the hostile Indian tribes. Captain Warren Cottle is given credit for many families following him to the Louisiana Territory, including the Farnsworth, Bailey, Ellis, Howard, Sanderson, Sears, Thomas, Simond, Turner, Woods, Keithley Allen, Power, and Emmon families. "The fact that, this fairly extensive number of people were willing to risk the many hazards of a journey into unknown, unsettled, and foreign country under the supervision of this one man, attest to the qualities of leadership and responsibility apparent in the character of Captain Warren Cottle." *The Lead Belt News*, Flat River, St. Francois County, Mo. Wed. June 2, 1965.

The caravan camped that winter on the Ohio River opposite Blennerhassett Island approximately three miles downstream from Parkersburg, West Virginia (part of Virginia prior to 1863). They followed the Ohio River which was the Mississippi's largest tributary, by volume, and flows through six states.

As soon as the river opened in the spring of 1800, the original caravan went down the Ohio to some distance below Cincinnati, near Louisville, slightly above the "Falls of the Ohio," where they left the river and struck out through the wilderness. They reached the Mississippi at Kaskaskia, traveled up the river to St. Louis, then on to St. Charles. Now before them lay the "promised land" that Captain Warren Cottle had seen earlier: The land along the Missouri.

Deacon Joseph Cottle, Warren Cottle's brother, and Joseph's son-in-law Zadock Woods settled near a spring in what is now Troy. Missouri, north of the

Dardenne and are credited with being Troy's founders. Woods Fort, named after Zadock, was built to protect the 25 to30 families that followed Joseph and Zadock to Troy. (See appendix) Joseph Cottle built the first horse-mill for grinding grain on the lot now occupied by the Lincoln County Motor Company. In 1803, Zadock Woods erected a double log house which kept a hotel and tavern.

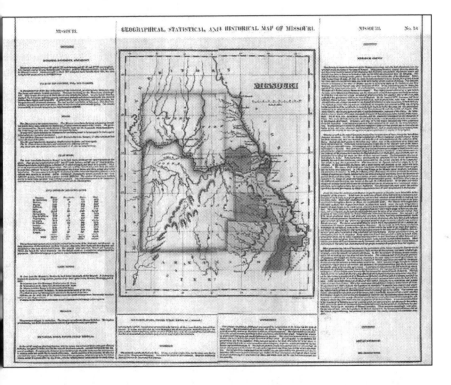

Other Cottles that settled along the Cuivre River in 1801-1803 were Issac, Joseph Sylvanus, Ira and Jonathan.

Chapter 3

The Beginning of American Settlements

"Among the early settlers on the Dardenne we may enumerate—Warren Cottle (1799), "ancient habitan des E.U." a native of Vermont; his son, Warren, Jr., was a physician and came with his father in 1799. Other sons of Warren, Sr., Ira, Stephen, and Marshall, also on this stream" (Note: he did not mention Oliver). Louis Houch, *A History of Missouri – from the Earliest Explorations until the Admission of the State into the Union*: (Lakeside Press, Chicago Volume II, 98. 1908)

* Capt. Warren Cottle, Sr. first came with his son Ira in 1798.

Early American settlers faced the Sac Dakota and Fox Indians, as well as the presence of Indians from Illinois who roamed a great area on both sides of the Mississippi River. They also faced the problems associated with "floating deeds" and the changing commandants. The number of American settlers was small; however, Daniel Boone, along with 15 families from Kentucky and the 40 families with Captain Warren Cottle, began the pioneer population growth of Missouri. Deacon Joseph

Cottle and son-in-law Zadock Woods also took many families and settled in the area that Warren Cottle had mapped in 1798 near the Cuivre River.

Cottleville's history as a settlement begins with the occupation by Warren Cottle Sr., his family and other early settlers near Dardenne River, which was obtained through Spanish-French land grants. "To the northwest of Green Bottom, along Dardenne Creek, settled members of the Cottle family, some of the few people from New England to arrive in the area during the colonial period" *National Historical Company*: (St. Louis, 1885), pp. 369, 453. Captain Warren built his home about one mile north of what is called Cottleville today. The first year was a challenge to the early settlers.

> "Down the hill from the house was a patch of corn in which pumpkins were planted. Day after day they watched the growth of the most forward of these, and when it was thought that they were ready, such was the effect of insufficient food, that two of the strongest men had to crawl up the hill, rolling the pumpkins before them." Clarence Edwin Carter, *Territorial Papers of the United States*, Vol. XIV, 1804-1814.

Marshall Cottle died that first year along with their child. Hannah wanted to go back to Vermont but stayed because she heard that her brothers David and Samuel Bailey, her sister Dorothy and several other Cottles were at Cahokia waiting to cross the Mississippi.

James Kerr, whose concession derived from Don Zenon Trudeau, Sept. 5, 1789, seems to have also been one of the first settlers along the Dardenne around 1799. John Coonz was granted land, Survey 285, for a plantation and mill on May 30, 1800. Adjoining John Coontz on the west was the settlement right of Peter and Rachel Teague on 640 arpents. Adjacent to them on the west was the concession of Nicholas Coontz as confirmed by Survey 58. The Georg Hoffman, Sr. Georg Hoffman, Jr. and Peter Hoffman families settled to the north, south, and west of the Cottle colony as confirmed in Survey 1787.

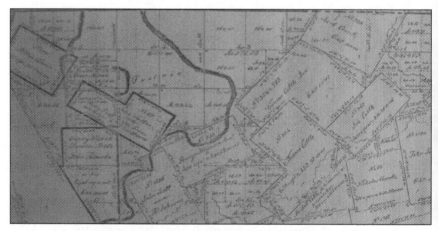

Spanish Land Grants ca. early 1800s as shown on Township 46.N.R.3.E Map Original found at St. Charles County Historical Society

Spanish land grants or "common fields" were given to numerous families as seen on early maps of the area. Spanish grants did not run perpendicular or "square" on maps.

The Minutes of the Land Commission include testimony that Warren produced a permit from Charles Dehault DeLassus, for him to settle dated Oct.8, 1799, and that this survey was certified on January 8, 1800. See Book 1 Page 400 Bok No. 3 Page 62 of the Recorders Office. Certificate No. 354. and 753. Warren received 650 and 522 arpents. An arpent is equivalent to .84 acre. Warren Jr. and Ira also received grants in Dardenne Township for 250 arpents and 353 arpents. Land Claim #304 (Capt. Warren Cottle) Land Claim # 354/753 (Dr. Warren Cottle, Jr.) Land Claim #353 (Ira Cottle) Land Claim #1776 (Nathaniel Simonds, as Marshall Cottle's Representative and husband of Marshall's Widow, Hannah Cottle) Book 4, page 223 and 355, Book 1, page 398, 399 and 400, Book 3, page 62 and 65, *Minutes of the Land Commission Relative to Land Grant Claims by Cottles*

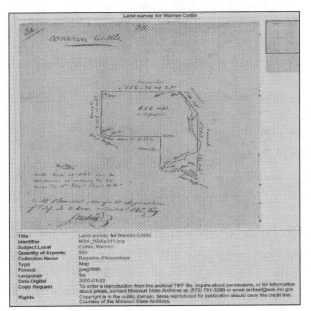

Land Survey for Warren Cottle
Image from the Missouri State Achieves

Dardenne Township occupied the central position of the county, and extended from the Missouri to the Mississippi rivers, embracing about 100 square miles. The following is a list of land owners in Dardenne Township, *History of St. Charles County p. 102*

James Kerr No. 1641 1020 arpents
Nicholas Coonse (Coontz, a Pennsylvania Dutchman No. 58 340, 980 arpents
Jacob Coontz No. 739 640 arpents
Peter and Rachel Teague No. 174 640 arpents
William Harrington
William McConnel No. 292 680 arpents
John McConnel No. 1785 640 arpents
Christian Wolf No. 948 640 arpents
Georg Hoffman, Sr. from Pennsylvania No. 1787 640 arpents No. 293 640 arpents
Peter Hoffman, from Kentucky No. 203 340 arpents, No. 57 255 arpents a miller
John Scott No. 1696 428 arpents
Charles Denny, a herb doctor and dentist as well as a mill owner
Teaque No. 174 640
Joseph Weldon No. 280 340
John Weldon No. 1,796 425 arpents
John Rourke No. 3225 260, 640 arpents
Milton and John Lewis No. 1771 299 arpents
David Miracle No. 168 340 arpents
Arend Rutgers No. 1669 5908 arpents, a Hollander, was one of the early settlers of Cottleville as well. He came prior to 1809, and afterwards built two water mills on Dardenne Creek a few miles west of the village.
Joseph St. Mary No. 2,526 160 arpents
John Smith No. 735, 640 arpents

Joseph Vosard No. 1,786 640 arpents
Tho: Howell No. 1798 640 arpents
Francis Howell No. 887 640 arpents (namesake of the
      Francis Howell School District in southeast St.
      Charles County)
John Howell No. 453 344 arpents
P. Hoffmann No.57 233 arpents
Nathaniel Simons No.1776 255 arpents
P. Chouteau No. 1704 433 arpents
Perry Brown No. 296 493 arpents
J. Beatty No 991 640 arpents
Grojean No. 480 170 arpents
Godfrey Krah No. 424 510 arpents
George Gatty No. 290 382 arpents
John Walker No. 67 340 arpents
Robert Spencer (namesake of Spencer Creek)
James Green (namesake of Green's Bottom) 800 arpents
Peter, Joseph and James Jerney
David Darst (namesake of Darst's Bottom)
Joseph and John Weldon (namesake of Weldon Spring)
John Zumwalt No. 296 493 arpents (namesake of Fort
      Zumwalt)
James Kerr No. 1641 1020 arpents
James Flaugherty 600 arpents
Jean Genereux
Joseph Langlois
John Parquette
Joseph Boshaut
Henry Schmidt
Christian Brandes
John Croft
John Teeter
John Adam Arras
John Castlio

"A goodly settlement around the site of present-day Cottleville in 1800 and 1801, and establishment of mills on the Dardenne by 1803, probably as early as 1801, widened the trail to a trace from the upper commons to the Dardenne and settlers west of the first crossing of that stream (Dardenne) had a well defined road as far as the site of the Pond Fort by the last mentioned date." *Missouri Historical Review* (The State Historical Society of Missouri July, 1933), Vol. 27, pp 307-314.

On December 12, 1803 John Coontz traded to Warren Cottle what was left of his saw and gristmills, recently damaged by the Dardenne's high waters, for the right to use them every fourth week when Cottle rebuilt them on the ford between his house and the land of Nicholas Coontz.

"... There is a bill from John Livingston for $25 for mason work in 1801 for work in establishing the mill therefore the mill was in operation for two years prior to this transaction. Early court records from 1811 states that Defendant took 50 lbs. of flour belonging to Christian Wolf from the mill of Warren Cottle. Some of the stone of the original mill can still be seen today in the town of Cottleville. "On the Dardenne Creek the mill that was taxed the highest in 1808 was the Warren Cottle Mill, valued at $400. His power for the mill came from an overshot wheel on the left side of the drop and it had wooden gears. The driving gear had all wooden cog wheels and the frame mill was one story high. On the Dardenne Creek mills were listed as owned by Mr. Coon, Denny, Rutger, Hoffmann, but the largest was owned by Cottle." *St. Charles Journal*, February 13, 1968.

The subscriber hereby notifies his customers and the public that he will sell at his mill on the Dardenne (Situated 3 Mi. from the Missouri Plank, as follows:
D. C.
Inch Oak, per 100 feet: 1   50
Do. Walnut Do.   200
The Missouri Gazette, Aug. 16, 1809 Warren Cottle.

"Cottle's grist mill used water power to sift and grind wheat oats, and other products. The water method proved to be superior to the other horse powered mills found within the county, and many people from around the area began to bring their harvested crops to Cottle's mill. Over the next decade, the large number of customers encouraged the establishment of small shops and lodges to accommodate those waiting, sometimes overnight, for their turn at the mill." *Architectural and Historic Resources Survey Report*, 2008.

Each generation of the Cottle family after Edward Cottle included at least one Cottle in the mill business. These mills were built adjunct to small dams erected of stone. The water stored behind the dams was then used to turn the wheels to grind grist.

Natural Spring in Cottleville located on Oak Street
Picture by Sheryl Guffey (2011)

This natural spring stonework can still be seen in Cottleville. The spring and the surrounding area provided a staging area for those waiting their turn at the mill.

In 1804, a country store, little hotels, and a wagon repair shop were built to accommodate the stranded travelers who tried to cross the Boone's Trail through the muddy conditions of the bottom lands. That same year, the Corps of Discovery, led by Captains Meriwether Lewis and William Clark, left St. Charles to discover regions further west using the Booneslick Trail.

Kountz's Fort, (Coontz's Fort or Koontz' Fort) was an early Indian fortification 10 miles west of St. Charles in the Cottleville area. The fort saw some of the first Indian outrages in North Missouri. The protection from this fort became more important when the Boone's Lick Trail, originally old Indian and animal trails, was routed through Cottle's property. The trail crossed the

Dardenne Creek near Warren Cottle's mill (now known as St. Charles Street) and was a major thoroughfare for early settlers using the mill and traveling westward. In 1807, Daniel Morgan and Nathan Boone traveled this trail, which was previously used in 1804 to guide the Lewis and Clark Expedition along this route.

"On his land near a large natural pond, rangers built the fort about 1808 to serve as protection against the Indians. Coonz established a tavern-stand, the first stopping place west of St. Charles on the Boonslick Road." Eugenia L. Harrison, *Place Names of Four River Counties in Eastern Missouri*. (M.A. Thesis, University of Missouri—Columbia, 1943). "Nathan Boone discovered a salt lick 150 miles west of St. Charles, and marked a trail from the Boone family land to the salt lick. The Boone's Lick Trail,-the first overland trail west was thus founded." Daniel T. Brown, Ph.D., *Newsletter from the Archives St. Charles Historical Society*, Vol. 11, Issue 5, August 2008.

Boone's Lick Road and Kountz' Fort Marker
Picture by Sheryl Guffey (2011)

In 1810, a mail stop was located within Kountz' Fort as settlers were now moving into the area. Indian attacks were frequent. The citizens in St. Charles County protested the inadequate defenses during the War of 1812 and asked Washington to send more troops. Their complaints were not adequately answered, and the settlers were forced to organize their own defense. They organized several companies of rangers, including The Boone Company, and were sometimes called "The Minute Men of the Frontier." Kountz' Fort played an important role in the protection of early settlers.

The area experienced a tide of immigration after the War of 1812. It is recorded in the CENSUS OF ST. CHARLES COUNTY, TERRITORY OF MISSOURI, 1817 AND 1819, by Oliver Howard, Indexer that there were "735 persons living in Dardenne Township in 1817, and 621 in 1819."

The Old Cottle brick home sat north of Cottleville above the Boone's Lick Trail, a route west from St. Louis for almost all overland travelers. Warren chose to build above fertile creek bottom land, with moderate hills on each side. "It was a well-built two story home of perfect colonial architecture with stone lintels, large fireplaces, with two large chimneys. Our records and newspaper clippings tell of a good deal of large social occasions held at the old Cottle home, large weddings, large family funerals, parties, and receptions." *St. Charles Journal,* April 16, 1964, as quoted in Schwabe, *"Ancestors and Descendants...,"* p.18. The Cottle mansion rose stately above the ever flowing Dardenne River (Creek)—the source of life since the introduction of Native Americans to the region. Initial inhabitants enjoyed this high ground, safe from floods. It also provided the best vantage for protection. The Cottle mansion stood where the ancient Indians had placed their homes—always on high ground. The Cottle mansion was located northwest of present day Warren Elementary School—which was named after Warren Cottle—and was the first brick house on the left at Weiss Road.

Present Day site of Warren Cottle Home of 1805, 567 Weiss Road

Warren Cottle Home (1805) Picture from The St. Charles County Historical Society (1960 Collection) Federal Style Home

**Oliver and Charity Cottle Home
on Land Grant 285, built ca. 1825**
Picture from The St. Charles County Historical Society (1960 Collection)

The walls are 2 ft. deep made of native stone. The main parlor fireplace mantel was a gift from Nathan Boone as a Thank you for extensive stays with Oliver. In 1815, Nathan Boone began construction of his new home at Temme Osage. Oliver Cottle's and Nathan Boones home were almost exact in layout and character. Nathan's walnut carved mantelpieces match the design in Oliver's home. Each had a full basement, a top floor ballroom and fireplaces in almost every room.

Visitors are welcome at the old Oliver Cottle home located at 4401 McClay Road. Today, the home has been transformed to serve as a wedding venue named Stone House of St. Charles.

Oliver built this home over a ten year period. He left the area to go to Texas in 1827 however died of yellow fever in New Orleans on his way. Oliver's brother, Ira, bought the 100-acre tract and home on May 13, 1833 and lived there briefly. Ira sold the home to William McClay. A feature article about the house, described it as follows:

> "The McClay house is known as one of the finest in St. Charles County, with its architectural charm of the last century. We visited and photographed the house and did, indeed, find it charming. It has a basement and three stories. The basement has a huge fireplace with an iron crane designed for cooking and food storage. The rock walls are two feet thick, such that rocking chairs could be used on the window sills." *St. Charles Journal*, February 2, 1961.

Elizabeth Thomas-Killam McClay, mother of Violetta Killam-Lorenzo's first wife and William McClay Picture from *The Cottle Genealogy,* compiled by Velma Cottle (Musick)

Ora and Elizabeth Keithly Cottle Home Picture from *The Cottle Genealogy*, compiled by Velma Cottle (Musick) (1965)

Ora, grandson of Captain Warren Cottle (brother to Lorenzo), and his wife Elizabeth lived in the Cottle home until 1880, when they moved to Wellsville. Ora Cottle became the mayor of Wellsville in 1885.

THE ORA COTTLE FAMILY
STANDING - LEFT TO RIGHT - HERMIE SCOTT, KING, ORLANA THOMAS
SEATED - LEFT TO RIGHT - MARY, LIZZIE (7 Yrs), ELIZABETH K. COTTLE,
ORA COTTLE, ADDIE (9 Yrs), WARREN

Ora Cottle Family

Cottle Home
Picture from the St. Charles County
Historical Society (1960 Collection)

Cottle Home Outbuilding
Picture from the St. Charles County Historical Society (1960 Collection)

Captain Warren Cottle died at his home in 1811 at the age of 56. He was buried in the cemetery named the Cottle Burying Ground, which is no longer in existence. It was on land owned by the Cottle family located near Hwy N. and Weis Road. In later years, the property was owned by the Drieswerd family.

Dr. Warren Cottle and Wife Salome

Dr. Warren Cottle, Jr., son of Revolutionary War hero Captain Warren Cottle, came to Missouri in 1799. However, in order to marry his first cousin Salome Cottle, he returned to Woodstock in 1801. Warren and Salome came back to Missouri, where he worked at the Cottle Mill as well as practiced medicine.

Dr. Warren Cottle was a collegiately trained physician. Historical records indicate Dr. Warren only practiced medicine relative to demand. However, it should not be said that he abandoned his profession. A review of his Probate Court file shows a great many bills for his medical services, many written in the French language. One patient's account:

> "Mr. Stoddard, patient –On 14 December 1821. The doctor traveled 12 miles and charged $6 for mileage, and three items of medicine. On that same date, he credited the patient's account for two heifers, $11 and 17 ½ pounds of cheese. His practice also included veterinary work and dentistry. "For too [sic] visits one too [sic] a little girl and the other to a negro. Both at five Dollars Eatch [sic]." *Missouri Historical Review,* The State Historical Society of Missouri V. XVII, No. 4, pp.308-309.

Dr. Warren, Jr. was also a soldier in the War of 1812. Warren enlisted in Captain Elijah Collard's Company of Infantry." The Company Pay Roll and Company Pay Muster Roll documents from the National Archives show Warren began service on February 17, 1812. Dr. Warren was appointed County Assessor by the newly elected Governor, Alexander McNair. (*St. Charles Journal,* 1821.) Dr. Warren was a Universalist and an earnest Whig throughout his lifetime.

The St. Charles County Court House probate records show that Dr. Warren died on his homestead in Dardenne Township and his wife Salome became the administrator. Dr. Warren Cottle passed to his heirs 992 acres of land, according to the tax list of 1836. Salome remained on the farm and reared the children, some of whom were very young. She died in 1845 at the age of 65. He and Salome were buried at the Cottle Burying Ground north of Cottleville, which no longer exists. See Appendix

THE PROBATE COURT FILE COVERING THE ESTATE OF SALOME COTTLE showed the inventory of the estate of Salome Cottle, dated October 8, 1847, divided her estate into two categories - "Cash," and "Other Property." The "Cash" portion showed that she had no money, as such; however she had two Notes as follows: 1) A note signed by Edward Cottle on June 20, 1847, of which $95, principal was still unpaid, along with interest at 6% for 110 days. 2) A note signed by M. Cottle on April 2, 1834, of which $65. Principal was unpaid, and interest for 13 years and six months. There was also $14.81 due from someone since November 1, 1836, plus interest for ten years and eleven months. The total value of this category was $238.92.

Salome's "Other Property" consisted of the following items:

ITEM	APPRAISED VALUE	ITEM	APPRAISED VALUE
1 Desk	$6.00	6 Chairs	$2.00
1 Bedstead	1.00	1 Kettle	1.25
1 Bedstead	.50	6 Pots & Skiliets	2.00
1 Table	1.50	1 Tea Kettle	not priced
1 Stand	1.00	1 Iron Hooped Tub	.50
1 Cupboard	5.00	1 Bay Horse	40.00
1 Clock	1.50	1 Yoke of Steers	25.00

Total value of this category of property was: $87.25

The total value of her estate, excluding land, was $326.17.

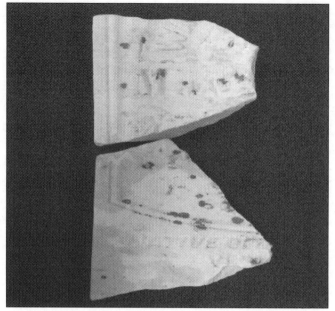

Broken Headstone of Warren Cottle
Dr. Warren Cottle, as described by Kate Greg in 1933 (Located in Cottleville City Hall).

Children of Dr. Warren Cottle (b. ca. 1780 d. 1823) and Salome Cottle, daughter of John and Elizabeth Cottle (b.1782 d. 1847) Dr. Warren and Salome Cottle named their children after characters in the Shakespeare play, "The Merchant of Venice."

Olive, b. ca. 1803 d. in early maidenhood

Alonzo, b. 1805 d. April 2, 1885, m. Mahala Turner November 23, 1834, d. April 17, 1848, Lived in Cottleville. They had six children: Charles, Helen, Olive, Lycurgres, Albro and Mahala. m. Elizabeth Palmer December 24, 1850, b. 1824 d. May 3, 1860 Cottle Burying Ground Elizabeth moved to Troy after the death of Alonzo leaving Lycurgres and Albro to be cared for by Ora.

Fidelo, b. 1807 d. in 1885
Move 1809-1850 to a daughter of Ira Cottle, 1809-1850, January 8, 1829

Alvora, b. August 7, 1809 d. after 1860 (attorney), m. Harriett Cottle, a daughter of Ira Cottle, January 8, 1829 Dardenne Township 1809-1850, m. Lydia Sitton November 3, 1853 moved to Troy 1850-1860, owned a 119 acre farm in Old Monroe, moved to California 1860-1881. Eight children: Emily, Malissa, Pauline, Olivia, Byron, Oliver, Z. Taylor and John

Lorenzo, b. September 13, 1811 d. September 26, 1892, m. Violetta Killam February 5, 1840 d. January 5, 1853 They had four children: Othello Julius, Sophrina, Edward and Oliver. m. Sarah Ann (Green) December 15, 1853, d. May 12, 1862 and had three children: Henry, Missouri Ann and an infant daughter that died m. Sarah (Barricklow) November 30, 1865, b. November 10, 1830, d. 1916

Pauline, b. 1815 m. Henry Bates California and had five children: John, Melinda, Solonan and Theodore and Laura. Moved to Sonoma County, California. Solonan died on the trip to California at the age of eight.

Ora, b. June 13, 1818 d. December 31, 1912, m. Elizabeth Keithly m. August 28, 1845 b. June 8, 1827 d. June

23, 1887 They had seven children: Samuel Warren S., Mary, Orlana, Hermie, King C., Addie Bell and Lizzie G. Lived in Cottleville then moved to Wellsville and became mayor and became a foster parent of Alonzo's children in 1885. Ora married Margret E. Turner in 1890 after Elizabeth's death in 1887.

<u>Otello</u> b. 1820, died young

Chapter 4

The Founding of Cottleville

The location of the Dardenne Creek and the proximity of the Boone's Lick Trail attracted many settlers to Dardenne Township. Interest in roads in general, and the Boone's Lick Road in particular, began for St. Charles County soon after the close of the War of 1812, when treaties with various tribes had allayed fear of Indian attack, and the tremendous tide of immigrants grew. The settlement by Warren Cottle was largely responsible for the routing of Boone's Lick Road through land settled by them. Boone's Lick Road passed through the lands of Captain Warren Cottle, Dr. Warren Cottle Jr., Oliver Cottle, and likely that of Ira Cottle. St. Charles County was organized October 1, 1812.

In 1820, Missouri statehood became a national issue. The "Missouri Compromise" allowed Missouri to enter the Union as a slave state and Maine as a free state, thus keeping the balance of slave and free states equal in Congress. Cottleville was located at 38 degrees 45'7" North, 90 degrees 39'12" West. The portion of the Louisiana Purchase area north of the 36-degree line was to be forever slave free. This distinction would cause Cottleville to become an area of conflict and decline in later years.

John Pitman started the avalanche of petitions on April 23, 1816, with a request signed by 12 property owners to have the road laid out from St. Charles to Dardenne Township. In the spring of 1819, Dr. Warren Cottle, Jr. presented a petition signed by 52 citizens around Dardenne to the road commissioners: Joseph Inks, Robert Prewitt, and Joseph Yardley.

An alternate petition was submitted routing the road to Franklin in Howard County. Yet another petition of 50 citizens was presented on November 26, 1827. Each petition indicated three distinct routes through the county. Nathan Boone, James H. Audrain, and Joseph Evans were appointed to make a report on the best route. A route was finally chosen in 1827, and was called the State Boonslick Road.

The story of Captain Lorenzo Cottle—the founder of Cottleville, the son of Dr. Warren Cottle, Jr. and the grandson of Captain Warren Cottle,—is extraordinary and reflective of the historical times of the early 19th century. The original town of Cottleville used 40 acres of land from Captain Warren Cottle and his son Marshall Cottle, who died one year after arriving in Missouri. Lorenzo inherited 200 acres of land from his father's estate in 1823 and became a farmer. Lorenzo was one of eight children to inherit land from Dr. Warren Cottle. At the age of 20, early in 1832, he enlisted under Nathan Boone in a company of mounted rangers for the Black Hawk War, and served 12 months.

"While on this expedition Mr. Lorenzo Cottle narrowly escaped being hopelessly separated from the command and losing his life, either by starvation or by falling into the hands of the Indians. He went out from the command a short distance to hunt, and becoming separated for them further than he expected, lost his "bearing" or the direction to take to reach them. He was not aware of his perilous situation until after he had killed a turkey and had started back to the command. After traveling quite as far as he thought was necessary, he still found no trace of his comrades, and it was impossible to rely on the following of their trail, for the whole country was checked with the trails of wild horses, Indians bands, and buffalo. Finally, giving up all hope of reaching them, he directed his course Toward Fort Gibson and expected to make the journey alone, if not prevented by starvation or overtaken by Indians. Coming down to a creek bottom on the way, he saw a cluster of saddled horses in the brush which he felt almost certain belonged to the Indians. At this sight his heart beat so fast and loud that he was almost afraid it would betray his presence to them. Slipping up stealthily to see, gun in hand, prepared to fight to the death rather than be taken alive, as soon as he got in full view, lo! He found they were his own comrades, and jumped so with joy that he almost split his boots. It is needless to say that he went on no more hunting excursions while on that expedition, and never afterwards has he had the fondness for hunting he had prior to his experience on the plains.

History of St. Charles County p. 164

Capt. Lorenzo Cottle returned home and farmed until the call of Missouri Governor Lilburn Boggs for volunteers for the Florida War (Second Seminole War) in the fall of 1837. Captain Cottle then enlisted in Capt. Jackson's company of mounted militia along with William Knott, William Fitch, Joseph Bozart, Joseph Welot, William Cordell-all from St. Charles County. History of St. Charles County p. 164 After the Missourians closed the Florida War by the brilliant victory of Lake Okeechobee on December 25, 1837 they returned to St. Louis and were honorably mustered out of service. Lorenzo was seriously wounded during the Battle of Lake Okeechobee while making the final charge against the Seminoles, when he was shot in the neck, breaking his collar bone.

Lorenzo Cottle Company Muster Roll Sheets from the Florida War 1837 and 1838

"Capt. Lorenzo Cottle was born on his father's original land grant on September 13, 1811. Lorenzo was only 12 years old when his father died. David W. Eaton, *How Missouri Counties, Towns, and Streams were Named*, Vol. XIII, No.1 (October, 1918), in which it is said of Lorenzo, "was raised on his father's farm near Cottleville, and received only a primary education, including reading, writing, arithmetic, etc, in the neighborhood schools of the period." "Capt. Cottle is one of the oldest living native born residents of the county, and is well known as one of the most highly respected citizens. He has served his country in two wars, but has rendered it even more valuable service as an industrious farmer and law-abiding citizen. In the years of his activity he accumulated considerable property and was the founder of the town of Cottleville, in this county (St. Charles). He still has a modest competence, and in the Indian summer of life is comfortably situate at his home in St. Charles. What is perhaps better still, a life of sobriety and good habits have preserved him in old age much physical vigor and his mental activity unimpaired-these, notwithstanding the hardships he endured in the pioneer days of the country and the exposures he underwent as a soldier of the republic in the swamps and everglades of Florida and in the malarial and then uninhabited regions of the upper Arkansas, the Red River, and the extreme South-west." Eaton, David W., "How Missouri Counties, Towns and Streams Were Named," in *Missouri Historical Review*, Vol. XIII, No. 1(October, 1918).

In 1839, Lorenzo bought a country store and proceeded to survey and lay out the town map of Cottleville, in memory of his father, Dr. Warren Cottle and his grandfather, Captain Warren Cottle. He created the township of Cottleville on his land, including the site of his store, and then sold and gave away a number of valuable lots. Lorenzo formally divided into small plots the town of Cottleville, which was designed in a grid pattern made up of 16 blocks with four, 60-foot wide plots on each block. This situated the community at the southern edge of his property.

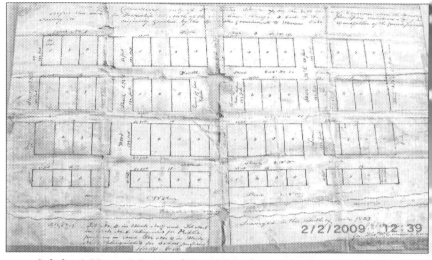

Original Map of Cottleville 1839 signed by Lorenzo Cottle
St. Charles County Historical Society Archives
Picture by Sheryl Guffey (2008)

Mr. Bill Popp, now deceased, and a retired archivist, and Sheryl Guffey rediscovered this map buried in the archival files at the St. Charles County Historical Society in 2008. This original signed map is drawn on the reverse side of a poster of President George Washington. Perhaps, paper was in short supply or Lorenzo was using American symbolism on his important document. It was truly an amazing find and restoration efforts have now preserved this historic map of Cottleville. It is interesting to note that on this map of 1839, Lorenzo shows the Dardenne River at the western most part of town.

Cottle's Mill was situated on the Dardenne River at the end of St. Charles Street and below Water Street. The amount of water flowing and flooding the area through the Dardenne bottom land was considerably more intense than it is today, allowing the mill to work with great efficiency. Today we know it as the Dardenne Creek, due to the waterway being rechanneled over a century later.

Reserved Plots for Public Use as drawn by Lorenzo Cottle
1839 St. Charles County Historical Society Archives
Picture by Sheryl Guffey (2009)

The streets of Cottleville retain today the same names as given by Lorenzo in 1839. Lorenzo made sure that, within the Original Town, there would be lots "reserved" for public usage. These areas included the lot at Oak Street and Second Street, the lot at Main Street (Hwy N) and St. Charles Street, and the lot across the street from this lot. It is also interesting to note that one of the streets is named after the Woods family. (Zaddock woods married Minerva Cottle, daughter of Deacon Joseph and Azubah Cottle)

**Lorenzo Cottle signature
on original Cottleville Town Map 1839**
The St. Charles County Historical Society Archives
Picture by Sheryl Guffey (2009)

Grant Map of 1861 St. Charles County Historical Society Archives
Darkened area shows the land donated for the town of Cottleville from
the original Spanish land grant.

Lorenzo married Violetta Killam, a daughter of
Elizabeth Killam, nee McClay, of St. Charles, Missouri
on February 5, 1840. Lorenzo and Violetta had four

children—Orthello, Sophronia, Edward, and Oliver—
between 1841 and 1849. Violetta died a short 13 years
into the marriage on January 5, 1853 at the age of 34.
Lorenzo had a successful business in Cottleville until he
retired from merchandising by selling out, in order to
resume farming. He relocated to a farm which he bought
in Lincoln County and lived there two years from 1845 to
1847.

Children of Lorenzo Cottle
and Violetta Killam (McClay)

Othello Julius b. May 8, 1841 d. March 3, 1909 buried
in Roff, Oklahoma; m. October 4, 1869 to Mary
Ellen (Teeter) Jamison d. March 4,1909. Lived in
Texas and fought in the Confederate Army, moved
to Oklahoma. Inherited Lot No.26 of a subdivision
of Lot No. 27 of Boons Survey. Their children all
moved to Texas or Florida

Orthello Julius Cottle
Picture from *The Cottle Genealogy* by Velma Cottle Musick

Julius Orthello Cottle and wife Mary
Picture from *The Cottle Genealogy* by Velma Cottle Musick

Sophronia Cottle Green and Irving Green
Picture from *The Cottle Genealogy* by Velma Cottle Musick

<u>Sophronia</u> b. 1843, m. Irving Green Inherited Lot #24
of a subdivision of Lot No. 27 of Boons Survey.
Moved to Texas and served in Stone's Regiment of
the Texas Calvary in the Confederate Army.

Edward Francis Cottle Tombstone - Oak Grove Cemetery
Picture by Sheryl Guffey (2010)

<u>Edward Francis</u>, b. September 12, 1846 d. April 5, 1915
Originally buried at the Cottle Burying Ground.

Oliver Thomas and Laura White Cottle
Picture from *The Cottle Genealogy* by Velma Cottle Musick

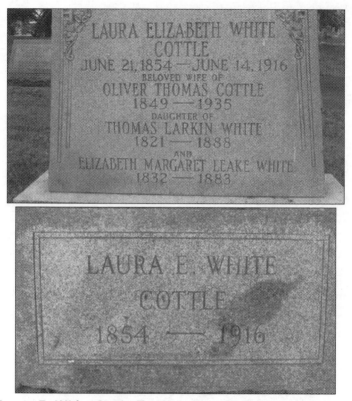

Laura E. White Cottle Tombstones - Oak Grove Cemetery
Pictures by Sheryl Guffey (2009

Oliver Thomas Cottle b. January 29, 1849 d. March 15, 1935 in Ashland, Kansas; m. Laura Elizabeth Cottle (White) b. June 21, 1854 d. June 14, 1916. Inherited Lots 4, 5, 27, 28, and 29 of Lot No. 27 of Boons Survey of the Commons.

Mary P. Daughter of L. & V. Cottle d. Dec.17, 1851 Unknown facts except for her name listed as one of the graves at the Cottle Burying Ground.

Lorenzo returned to Cottleville in 1847. He had a real estate value of $7,350, personal property valued at $2,975, and owned two slaves: one 50-year-old female and a 14-year-old male 4. Capt. Lorenzo Cottle had two farms in the county, which he rented. He was a conservative Democrat and a Universalist. Lorenzo married Sarah Ann Green, daughter of James and Rachel Green (Yanel) on November 30, 1853. Sarah Ann died on May 12, 1862 at the age of 33.

Children of Lorenzo and Sarah Ann Cottle (Green) born 1829 died May 12, 1862

Henry A. Cottle b. 1850 d. September 10, 1851 (1 Year 1
    Month and 24 days) Cottle Burying Ground
Missouri Ann "Matilda" b. April 20, 1855 d. July 18, 1875;
    m. Fowler unknown. Cottle Burying Ground

Lorenzo then resided at "Hotel 8th Class," in Cottleville, where he was an innkeeper from 1864 to 1865. Lorenzo married again on November 30, 1865 to Sarah M. Cottle (Barricklow), who was born in Indiana on November 10, 1830 but moved to St. Charles County in 1839. Sarah's first husband was Jerome Coonan, who died in 1857. Lorenzo and Sarah lived in Cottleville and continued farming until 1876, but did not have any children. Lorenzo and Sarah M. then moved to St. Charles and lived on Jefferson Street. They owned a broom factory and 10 town lots for some six years, but in 1883 Lorenzo retired from all regular business due to a stroke that produced some paralysis. In 1892 Lorenzo died of old age and was buried at Oak Grove Cemetery. Sarah M. survived Lorenzo for 24 years.

Lorenzo Cottle

**Lorenzo Cottle and Sarah M. Cottle Grave Marker
next to his Grandfather Captain Warren Cottle, Sr.
– Oak Grove Cemetery**
Picture taken by Sheryl Guffey (2010)

Major John Pitman, another Revolutionary War Hero, came to Cottleville from Kentucky in 1810 and settled about one-half mile west of the town proper, north of the Dardenne Creek. He purchased the farm from George Hoffma, who owned part of the property ceded to the Cottles. The Hoffmans lived next to the Cottle family. In 1812, Congress made the territory of Missouri to avoid confusion with the recently admitted state of Louisiana. John Pitman, along with Robert Spencer were elected to represent the people of the District.

Pitman House - Cottleville

John Pitman and his son, David K. Pitman, both played an important role in Cottleville's development. In 1821 John Pitman was commissioned colonel of the Fifteenth Missouri State militia. John eventually moved to Montgomery county where he served as county judge for a number of years. John Pitman died January 1, 1839 at the age of 85 and was buried in the Pitman Cemetery between Hwy N and Interstated 364. There are 18 grave sites in the Pitman Cemetery, one dating back to 1811.

David Kyle Pitman was born December 20, 1805 in Kentucky and came with his family to the area at the age of five. David Kyle married Caroline L. Hickman (July 1, 1805-October 15, 1852) and had four children: Richard, Lydia, Caroline, and John. After Caroline died, he then married Eliza Hamilton Baker (May 25, 1813-March 19, 1887). David K. Pitman added the First Addition and Second Addition to the original town map of Cottleville and the donation of land for public use, south of the original plat set out by Lorenzo Cottle. (Note: A plat was a Middle English term for a plot of land.)

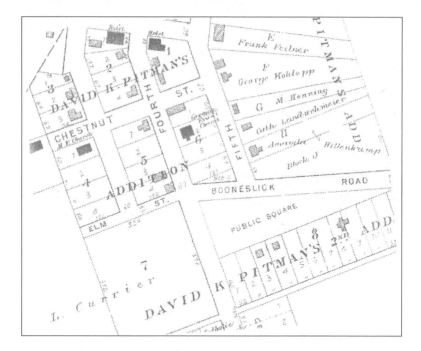

David died October 13, 1891 and was buried in the J. Pitman Burial Grounds. The Lindemann family lived in the Pitman house for many years; however, the original house no longer exist.

Chapter 5

The Development of Cottleville

Cottleville became truly established in 1843, when the first "official" U. S. mail stop was created. Cottleville thrived mainly due to its location, one day's journey from St. Charles and the Missouri River. The floods and muddy flood plains west of Cottleville made passage very hard and many travelers remained in town. Over half of the population was of German descent by 1850 and they held strong to their beliefs about the issues of prohibition and slavery. It is interesting to note that the city of St. Charles was not incorporated until March 10, 1849, 10 years after Cottleville was plotted by Lorenzo Cottle. "Cottleville apparently was very prosperous and in 1846 it was listed as having two hotels, eleven businesses, and a population of 500 people." Edna McEthiney Olsen, *Historical Series.*

In 1846, Cottleville became a rival of St. Charles, with petitions circulated to have the County Seat of Justice transferred from St. Charles (First State Capital of Missouri) to Cottleville. It was signed by the required three-fifths of Cottleville's taxable residents.

Transcribed Petition of 1846
by Sheryl Guffey (2009)

Original Signature Page of 1846 Petition
St. Charles County Historical Society Archives

The original document is four pages in length.

"The scheme to move the county seat failed, but what if it had not? Perhaps St. Charles would today be a sleepy little town on the Missouri and Cottleville would be a thriving city, rather than a peaceful hamlet in the country." *Community News*, Vol.1 No.26, March 7, 1962.

The 1848 Land and Property Records show some of the major landowners within Cottleville included: Ferdinand Massey/Massy/Massa, Christopher Bauer, David K. Pitman, Frederich Busch, Nicholas Coons, Alonzo Cottle, Mahala Cottle, Warren Cottle, Alvora Cottle, Lorenzo Cottle, Ira Cottle, Violetta Cottle, Frederick Rohland, Arnold Krekel, Franz Krekel, Franz Krekel, Adam Arras, Margaretha Arras, Reinhard Kundere, Jon S. Streib, Jon Bottell, John Hahn, Hieronimus Hoermann, Daniel Schneider, Conrad Berthold, Heinerich Rüffer, Martin Miller, Hiram Castlio, James Bacon, Cristoph Wagner, Edward Cunningham, Martin Estel, John Hackman, Melehiah Baldridge, Susan Baldridge, William Baldridge, James Baldridge, Samuel McCluer, John Doan, James Green, Hezekiah King, Wyllys King and John Warburton.

A "public" one-room school existed in the Cottleville area as early as 1815. However, in 1851, David K. and Eliza H. Pitman sold property to Garret Altvater and Alden Parnsworth, as trustees of the Cottleville School District, for $30 to build a new school.

One Room Schoolhouse #3 (1873) at 5546 Chestnut Street
Picture at the St. Charles County Historical Society

Schoolhouse #3 was built ca.1873 and served as a school until the 1950s. In 1941, Cottleville School District was voluntarily annexed to the St. Charles County Consolidated School District No. 2 and its successor Reorganized School District No. III., which is now the Francis Howell School District.

Schoolhouse #3 Picture taken by Sheryl Guffey (2009)

The one-room school house building was renovated for residential use by Clara Lindemann in the 1970s, but no longer remains. It was torn down in 2017.

One Room Schoolhouse Students

The students in the photo are, from left: (back row) Russell Kasper, Evelyn Boenker, LaVern Lauer, and Dorothy Hoffman; (third row) Clifford Dingledine, Winston Wolf, Calvin Phillips, June Kasper, Violet Conoyer, Esther Wolf, Leola Huestman, Maurice Merx, and Virgil Lauer;

(second row) Virginia Dingledine, unknown, Ruth Kessler, Ruby Conoyer, Margie Lee Hillenkamp, Marcella Mother(s)head, Bernice Gutermuth, Gladys Wolf, Jackie Kasper, Robert Conoyer, Lorrain Jennings, and Ella River (teacher); (front row) Robert Jennings, Marlin Phillips, Ed Wolf, Elroy Jennings, and Orville Fehr.

I met with Ruth Lauer (Vierling) one afternoon in April of 2011. Ruth is the granddaughter of Sigmund Kessler, who at one time owned a 177- acre farm in Cottleville, and was the daughter of George Valentine and Talitha Kessler. George had a garden in the exact location that my father gardened when he bought the property in 1970. In 1857, the Kesslers owned what was called Krekel Camp and much of the southern edge of Cottleville, as well as property all the way to Marthasville. Louis Houpt married Clara Kessler, who died in 1877, and then remarried to Christina Fehr. Louis was a member of Colonel Krekel Post No. 4 and the Insurance Lodge of Cottleville around 1888. The Kesslers built a house in 1918 on Gutermuth Road, which still stands today and is occupied by Mary Crawford. Ruth knew everyone of her classmates in the picture above. She told me that Marcella spelled her name Mothershead and that the road in Cottleville was misspelled Motherhead.

"Cottleville's first post office <u>building</u> was built in 1843." Hayden Goodwin *Postal Guide: County Atlas*, 1875. There were about 500 residents living in Cottleville at this time. The Butterfield Overland Stage began in Tipton, Missouri and may have run through Cottleville under several names. The stage coach and mail delivery stop depot was built on the Boone's Lick Road and was located on the hill property by the Cottleville Fire Department. The blessings came for Cottleville by creating a stopping spot for travelers, due to the muddy bottom lands, mail service, and better roads. Many hotels sprang up and visitors used horse-and-buggies to get to the depot. The Boone's Lick Road became a state road in 1851.

"Cottleville is recorded as a site of Yellow Fever and Cholera in 1851." *The Society of the New York Hospital, March 1989. Letters on Yellow Fever, The Cholera and Quarantine by Alexander F. Vache, M.D.*

A corporation was formed under the name of the St. Charles and Western Plank Road Company, for the purpose of constructing a plank road from the city of St. Charles, along the Boone's Lick Road to the western end of the county on February 27, 1851. About $34,000 worth of stock was subscribed and a timber plank road was built from St. Charles westward along the Boone's Lick Road as far as - North of Cottleville. The toll road of two bits (25 cents) was known as the Western Plank Road and it did increase the population of Cottleville for the 13 years it existed. The 9 mile road project ultimately failed because of the continued maintenance cost, the planks warped and rotted, and because the wooden planks were often stolen for use as building materials.

Today you can still see where the bridge by Hwy N at Eagle Hill Lane was originally. The Western Plank Road turned on to N by the Cottleville Fire House and dropped down to the bottom land using St. Charles Street, then across.

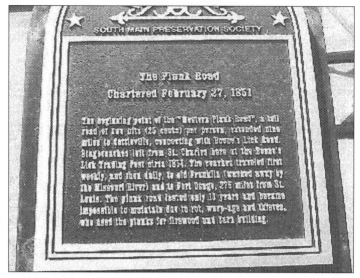

Western Plank Road Marker in St. Charles Picture by Sheryl Guffey (2010)

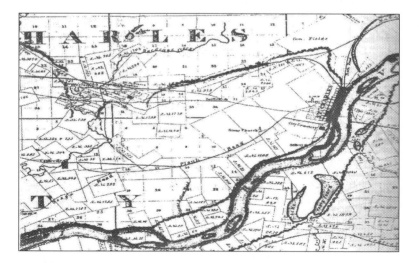

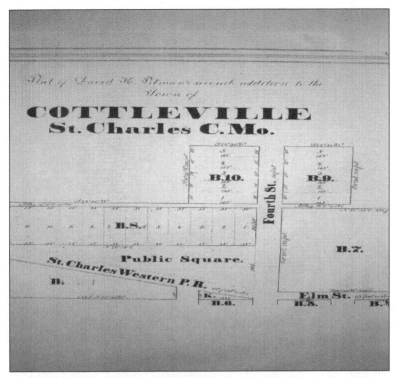

Western Plank Road Map Maps at the St. Charles County
Historical Society

Chapter 6

Church History

Cottleville was rare in that it had Protestant German, Negro Baptist, and Catholic congregations. In 1852, David K. Pitman deeded a tract of land in the center of town to the Methodists and the Southern Methodist Church was built in 1854 at a cost of $1600. The constituent members were William C. Ellis, S. R. Watts, James T. Sanford, R. H. Pitman and David K. Pitman with 20 members in total that year. The pastors who served this congregation were Rev. E.M. Muron, R.N.T. Holliday, J. F. Riggs and William Penn.

Cottleville First Church - Southern Methodist (1854)
Picture from the Cottleville Calendar (1970)

Lilburn Dotson, Current Owner
Picture by Sheryl Guffey (2011)

*****

David K. Pitman donated another tract of land to the south of town for a Negro Baptist Church, cemetery, and school. "Cottleville has four stores, three grocery, two hotels, four shoemakers, two carpenters, one butcher, two public schools (white and colored), post office, two churches (Evangelical & Methodist). A Catholic Church is about to be built." *The St. Charles Cosmos,* March 6, 1873.

African School Picture from St. Joseph's Church Dedication Booklet (1962)

1905 Plat Map of Cottleville St. Charles County Historical Society Archives

The African Church and School was built before the Civil War in about 1852.

*****

The Evangelical faith established itself in Cottleville as early as 1850. Reverend Adolph Baltzer began making trips to Cottleville preaching at their public school and homes. The Reverend Peter Goebel, who was the pastor of Friedens Church, preached at Cottleville occasionally and became the founding pastor of St. John's Deutsche Evangelische Gemeinde in 1866. A group from Weldon Spring decided that the church should be moved and for several years the congregation met in a one-room log cabin built on the Christian Fey farm near Weldon Spring. Rev. J.J. Hotz, born in Switzerland, was the first resident Church Pastor and served from 1866 to1868, traveling from Cottleville to Weldon Spring.

A group of people in Cottleville began calling themselves Free Protestant and organized under the name Unabhaenige Evangelical Protestant Gemeinde. A cleavage developed in the Weldon Spring congregation and many members united with the Free Protestant group in Cottleville.

> "During the years 1865 and 1866, the following children were baptized: Johan Wilhelm, Miller, Carl Andreas Miller, August Jacob, Tuchman, Leonean, Emil Kessler, Luisa Ema Schneider, Maria Christine Luise Stephan, John Nikolas Kohlepp, Maria Dorothea, Elisabeth Sidentop, Ana Bertha Fey, John Heinrich Pfeiffer, Ana Luise Wahlbrink, Eva Katharina Wolf, Anna Maria Elizabeth Glock, Augusta Debertsheiser, Johanes Pfeiffer, Charles Arres, Edward Heinrich Pharr, Rosina Magaretha Peter.

There were two weddings- John Huser and Elisabeth Benkert and John Herman Ermeling and Marie Berning. Adam Gutermuth, Katherina Elisabeth Pfeiffer, Anna Maria Schneider and Elisabeth Gutermuth were confirmed."

Pastors at St. John's Deutsche Evangelische Gemeinde, Unabhaenige Evangelical Protestant Gemeinde, and St. John's United Church of Christ:

Independents	1868-1873	Rev. Paul Quarder	1906-1907
Rev. G. Doernenburg	1873-1875	Rev. Oscar Krafft	1908-1908
Rev. R. Henschel	1875-1877	Rev. G. Bohnenstengel	1908-1910
Rev. F. W. Adomeit	1877-1880	Rev. A. H. Bockstruck	1910-1916
Rev. Daniel Irion	1880-1885.	Rev. Dr. Gaston Bach	1916-1917
Rev. W. Buehler	1885-1886	Rev. H. Thomas	1917-1919 (of St. Charles)
Rev. W. Fitsch	1886-1887	Rev. E. C. Brink	1920-1938 (of Weldon Spring)
Rev. Ph. Albert	1887-1889		
Rev. Peter Goebel	1889-1901		
Rev. S. Gonser	1901-1905		
Rev. Wm. Cramm	1938-1940		
Rev. Roy Winkelmann		1940-1942	

Rev. Martin Torbitsky	1942- 1946
Rev. Theodore Haefle	1946-1948
Rev. Stanley E. Anderson	1948-1950
Rev. Laurin Detweiler	1950-1954
Rev. Louis Hammann	1954-1956
Rev. Carl E. Gabler	1957-1963
Rev. Robert Schmidt	1964

St. John's United Church of Christ 1866-1966 Anniversary Booklet,

(September 11, 1966)

John Rupp, Adam Merx, and John Huser purchased a saloon and dance hall building located on Lot 2 and 1/2 of Lot 3 of Block 6 of the Pitman Addition on September 9, 1870 for the Cottleville church. On September 18, 1871, this piece of property was deeded for $1,500 with Phillip Vierling, Adam Woherle, and Fred Dreder acting as trustees. Windows and doors were purchased from St. Joseph's Parish. In 1873, they reorganized and the church was called "Deutsche Evangelische St. Paul's Germeinde Zer Cottleville." The Weldon Spring church adopted the name "Evangelical Emmanuel" and eventually the Cottleville church adopted the name "St. John's Evangelical Zer Cottleville."

St. John's United Church of Christ 1870 Picture from St. John's United Church of Christ 1866-1966, *100th Anniversary Booklet, September 11, 1966*

Bertha Frese sold one-half of Lot 3 to the church for $1.00 and a small one-sided steeple was built around 1895. In 1900 the steeple was rebuilt and then rebuilt again after lighting had struck it. The church became the Knights of Columbus Hall in the 1960s until they rebuilt further north off of Hwy N. The original church building was mostly torn down and became Mannino's Meat Market and Jo's Bar. St. John's United Church of Christ built a new parsonage in 1964 on ground donated by the Henry Pfeiffer family, located at 945 Wolfrum Road.

United Church of Christ Cemetery
The cemetery was originally known as the Camp Krekel Civil
War Training Ground. St. John's cemetery has approximately 420
headstones from the 1870s to present.

*****

Franciscan priests traveled by train from St. Louis to St. Peters and then by horse-and-wagon to Cottleville during the 1850s. Father Christopher Wapelhorst of All Saints Parish in St. Peters occasionally held masses for 35 Catholic families in an unoccupied farm house belonging to Thomas Croft. This house was located on what is now the picnic grounds of the parish. Fr. Wapelhorst encouraged Catholics in Cottleville to organize a parish of its own. John Seymour, a grocer of Cottleville, and John Fitz, a farmer living in the Weldon Spring area, were authorized to solicit funds.

Seymour and Fitz successfully secured $1,700 in pledged funds and a tract of land was purchased from David K. Pitman for $250 in 1864. It was decided to build a brick building with a limestone foundation. Window frames and doors were purchased from St. Lawrence O'Toole Church in north St. Louis for a cost of $6.00 each. Unfortunately, Father Wapelhorst was transferred to Wisconsin and building of the church ceased. Some of the building material was returned and the windows and doors were sold to the Evangelical congregation. The next nine years proved hard for the Catholics in Cottleville until Father Eberhardt Gahr arrived and began obtaining pledges once again. He was able to collect $1,500, but became ill with malaria.

"Success came at last in the spring of 1874, after five leading men of Cottleville went to St. Louis and made an agreement with the Archbishop to build a church and residence for a priest. "Sandy Hence, *Heritage Treasures: Beginnings of St Joseph's Parish, Cottleville,* St. Charles County Historical Society, 2006.

**Jon Buse, Anton Hoester, Francis Menne, J. George Pfaff
and Bernard Menne Jr.**
Picture from St. Joseph's Church Dedication Booklet,
September 16, 1962

These men collected $2,000 in pledges, removed the original foundation and designed a smaller, less pretentious church.

St. Joseph Catholic Church was built on land that had formerly been owned by Joseph Reisdorff, Frank Fehr, Thomas Croft, John Seymour, and David K. Pitman. Local men built a large two-story, wood frame house with the church sanctuary upstairs and living quarters for the new priest on the main floor using the $2,000 of pledged money. In six months, the project was completed and Father Ferdinand Borgmeier came from St. Louis to celebrate Mass. It took two years for the Archdiocese of St. Louis to appoint the first resident priest.

Interior of 1ˢᵗ Church built in 1874 Dedicated by Reverend Ferdinand Borgmeier
Picture from St. Joseph's Church Dedication Booklet, September 16, 1962

"By 1876, Cottleville had eleven stores, two hotels, two carpenter shops, two public schools (one colored) and three churches, Evangelical, Methodist and Catholic." Sarah Hense, *Heritage Treasures: The Beginnings of St. Joseph's Parish, Cottleville* (2006).

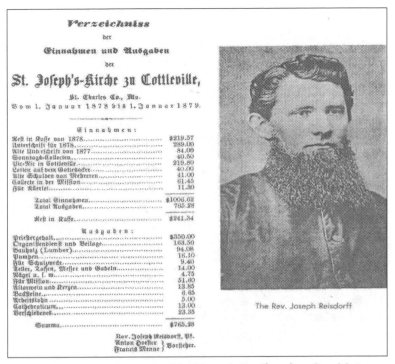

The Rev. Joseph Reisdorff

Images from St. Joseph's Church Dedication Booklet
(September 16, 1962)

In 1876, Father Joseph Reisdorff became the congregation's first resident priest. Father Reisdorff was fluent in German and proved a great asset for the German-speaking community. German immigrants comprised two-thirds of Cottleville's population by 1890. Father Reisdorff served 10 years. It has been presented that local Protestants objected to his playing cards and drinking beer on Sunday with parish families. In 1877, two large bells were purchased for the bell tower and these bells can still be seen in the new church today.

St. Joseph Parish Old Bell Tower built in 1874
Picture taken in 1904, from St. Joseph's Church Dedication Booklet,
September 16, 1962

Father Schmidt of Dardenne parish served Cottleville for six years (1887-1893). Father Schmidt resigned and Father Hundhausen (first name unknown) then arrived and led the congregation and taught school (1895-1900). Father Hundhausen was thrown out of a buggy and was seriously hurt and no longer could administer to the needs of his parish. Father Julius A. Schultz arrived in 1900 and served nine years.

**Fr. Julius A. Schultz and his
First Communicants ca. 1900-1909**
Picture from The St. Joseph's Church Dedication Booklet,
September 16, 1962

Father Striewe then served 15 years (1910- 1925), in which he was able to see the completion of a new brick church, built again by local men. The estate of John Toelle left $1,200 for the building of a new church, which was used for 47 years.

St. Joseph Church in 1914   St. Joseph Church in 1961
Original Photos are at The St. Charles County Historical Society

Father Range then served seven years (1925-1932) and saw a six-room rectory built. In 1932, Father William Pezold took over the parish and remained there until his death in 1977 at the age of 84. Father Pezold obtained the teaching services of three Sisters of the Most Precious Blood from O'Fallon and the first church of 1874 was renovated. Father Pezold drove a Chevy to pick up students, six at a time, so that they could attend school at St. Joseph.

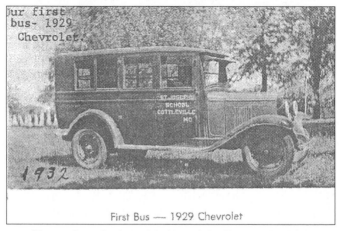

First Bus —— 1929 Chevrolet

Picture from St. Joseph's Church Dedication Booklet, September 16, 1962

The school grew and in 1938 a new school was erected at a cost of $16,000, even though this was in the time of the Great Depression. Father Pezold was also instrumental in the creation of public housing in Cottleville for the workers at the Weldon Spring Ordinance Plant. Father Pezold got the bank of O'Fallon, the owners of a 35-acre plot, to subdivide and sell the parcels to plant workers for $50. He then had new homes built from wreckage at the plant and eventually had 24 new homes erected. Father Wenceslaus Svehla, at the age of 70, came out of retirement in 1942 to assist Father Pezold until his death.

Fr. Wenceslaus Svehla and Fr. William Pezold
Picture from the St. Charles County Historical Society Archives

After 96 years, the first church's foundation cracked and was remodeled to serve as a convent. Eventually, the old convent was torn down and a new brick rectory was built in its place. In 1961, a new church was built at a cost of $200,000. Father Maguire came to St. Joseph Catholic Church in 1970 and a new school was built. Father Griesedieck then came to preach in 1976.

Monsignor Whited took the reigns in 1988 and led St. Joseph Catholic Church until 2004. The parish grew to approximately 4,500 families in the parish and become the largest in the archdiocese. In 2004 Monsignor James Callahan was appointed to lead the parish and has successfully continued the growth. Monsignor Callahan saw the parish debt of 5 million dollars retired in just 4 ½ years.

Shortleaf Pine (Pinus echinata) surrounding the St. Joseph Church Cemetery Picture by Sheryl Guffey (2011)

This pine species, is the only native pine tree in Missouri and is rarely seen this far north.

St. Joseph Catholic Church Built in 1999
Picture from City of Cottleville Architectural/
Historic Resource Survey (2008)

St. Joseph School picture by Sheryl Guffey (2011)

Chapter 7

Cottleville 1853-1900

The City of Cottleville was incorporated in 1853; however, Cottleville did not prosper as much as other local towns, as Boone's Lick Road became of less importance. Railroads and major transportation infrastructure was built elsewhere in the county and Cottleville government went dormant for many years.

David Kyle Pitman created two subdivisions on his land which created new housing growth. The first bordered the original blocks plotted by Lorenzo, parallel to the Western Plank Road. The second addition was south of Boonslick Road. There were about 350 residents of Cottleville.

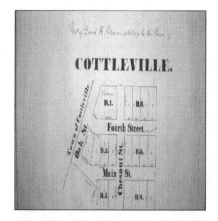

Pitman Addition 1856
Maps at the St. Charles County Historical Society

The Civil War erupted in 1861 and Cottleville became a Union stronghold. In 1861, the debate over secession raged in Missouri and the General Assembly called for a convention. There were to be three delegates from each senatorial district and almost 700 people attended a meeting in Cottleville. Enlistments for the Union were numerous and the St. Charles County "Home Guard" had 1,300 men, composed primarily of Germans and known as "Krekel's Dutch." Camp Krekel was used for Union military drill maneuvers during the Civil War. Arnold Krekel founded the *St. Charles Democrat*, was instrumental in railroad placements, and he laid out the town of O'Fallon, Missouri. Camp Krekel was situated near what is now the site of St. John's United Church of Christ Cemetery and the Missouri American Water Company on Motherhead Road.

When you visit the Cottleville Wine Seller, you will see a grave marker that was discovered on the property. It leans against a tree in the courtyard. It is hard to read, however it reveals the names of Christian Brandis and his wife Sofie.

Christian was born 1801 in Germany, was naturalized and died in the year 1867. He served in the German Regiment, St. Charles Missouri Home Guard as a Private.

"The County Convention of the Radical Union Party took place in Cottleville on September 7, 1864 and resolved in favor of preservation of the Union, support of Thomas C. Fletcher for governor and complete abolition of slavery," Steve Ehlmann, *Crossroads: A History of St. Charles County* (2004), pp. 86, 94. The Civil War had a major impact on Cottleville and the Cottles were right in the middle of the conflict, as were so many families.

David Pitman sold the Catholic Church property to build the Church directly across from Krekel's Camp.

Dardenne Creek ca. 1860s
Picture provided by Judith Kuhl (2011)

The North Missouri and Eastern Kansas Business Directory of 1867-1868 listed Cottleville as having about 340 inhabitants. Land records near the town of Cottleville from 1861-1880 show the property holders, which included: Warren Cottle; Ora Cottle; Lorenzo Cottle; Nicholas Coontz; John Scott; George Arras; Herman Hein Wehmeier; Clarence and Blanche Kessler; Charles and Caroline Lauer; Alma F. Lauer (Fehr); F.F. Fehr; John, Adam and Sophia Gutermuth; John and Suzanna Tidemann; George Huffman; John Rourke; Milton Lewis; James Kerr; Francis Howell; Arend Rutgers; Christian Wolf; William McConnell; John McConnell; Peter Teayne; Jacob Coontz; Oliver Cottle; Pauline Kappeller; George Kohlenhofer; Sigmund Kessler; Joseph Zerr; Michael Pfaff; Daniel Sammuelmann; Rudolph Hillenkamp; Otto Deberthause; John Pitman; John Toelle; Henry Pieper; Francis Keene; Daniel Stephens; Benjamin Emmons, Reinhard and Elizabeth Kunderer, H. and Christine Wehmeier. Jr, Joh and Eva Streib, and Gertrude Hanne.

Other property holders mentioned in the these records included: Louis Houpt (who first married Clara Kessler, then married Christina Fehr); Johann M. Phillips married Rosetta Fehr, 1846 who had nine children, Elizabeth, Joh, Louis, William, Emma, George, Edward, Charles, and Joseph; Lizzie Merx; Johann M. Phillips (Farmer and Stock-raiser, Cottleville, 1846), who married Rosetta Fehr; Dr. J. C. Edwards (Physician, Cottleville, 1853), who married Sarah A. Pritchett in 1854, died in 1873 later married Sallie Stone in 1874 and had one child, died 1875 and then married Kate Stone (sister to Sallie in 1880; Jacob Keiser (Dealer in General Merchandise and Post Master, Cottleville, 1857), who married Emma Morgerkort in 1880 and had one child, John Hoffman (Farmer, Cottleville, 1860), who married Mary Schiller and had 10 children: Issac, Mary, Elizabeth, Katie and George (twins), Laura, Alexander, Henry, Rosa and Ella; and, John Hendricks (Blacksmith), who lived on David K. Pittman's property.

Dr. Herman Baltzer (Physician, 1875) married Eva Hartmann in 1876. He lived and practiced medicine at the location of the current. He then built one block away and the original house and separate office still stands today. Dr. Baltzer was also Clerk of the School Board and was very interested in the cause of education. Dr. Herman Baltzer's father was Rev. Prof. Adolph Baltzer, the minister of the Evangelical Friedens Church and sometimes preached in Cottleville. Dr. Baltzer's mother was Louisa Van Laer. Rev. Daniel Irion (Pastor of the Evangelical Church, Cottleville, 1877) married Friederica Stanger and had three children: Oscar, Rudolph and one deceased. John C. Binkert (Binkert & Eohleghnhoepheir, Dealers and General Merchants, 1883), who married Mary Marks in 1878 and had one child, Ida K.; and, Julius and Simon Baer (Storeowners, Cottleville, 1890), who eventually becoming partners in Stix, Baer and Fuller Department Stores.

There was economic prosperity at the turn of the 20th century as more efficient farming was available and roads were improved. The first railroad bridge to span the Missouri River was opened to traffic in May 1871; however, Cottleville saw little impact from the expansion of the railroad infrastructure and new major roadways. Cottleville also was a meeting place for the Liberal Republicans, who called for reform, peace, and insight. They expressed their dislike for Ulysses S. Grant, who was reelected as President of the United States as a Republican in 1872.

Cottleville boasted multiple doctors, general strores, blacksmiths, shoemakers, wagon makers and saloons. By 1873, 87% of the population of Cottleville was either from Germany or of German descent.

Right to left first row: Samuel Warren Cottle (1846-1921), Addie Belle Cottle (1863-1920), Ora Cottle (1818-1912), Elizabeth Cottle (1827-1887), Lizzie Cottle (1867-1928), Mary Cottle (1848-1931).
Right to left second row: Orlana Cottle (1852-1915), King C. Cottle (1856-1915), Hermie Cottle (1854-1939)

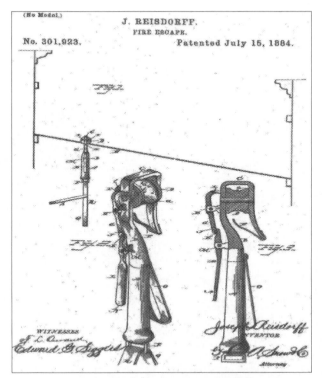

Joseph Reisdorff of Cottleville
Patent No 301,924 for a Fire Escape
Image from the United State Patent Office (1884)

Chapter 8

Historic Buildings

There are 12 buildings built before 1900 that still exist in the historic district of Cottleville according to the Recorder of Deeds for St. Charles County.

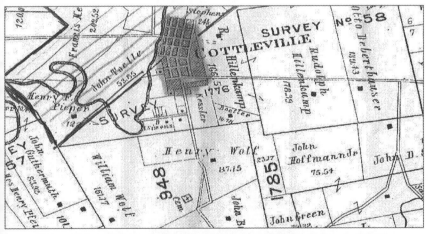

Townships 45 & 46 North Range 3 East Plat Book 1905
St. Charles County Historical Society

**5212 4ᵗʰ Street-Hwy N (Built in 1841
and reconstructed in 1912)**
Picture from City of Cottleville Architectural/
Historic Resource Survey (2008)

This building was owned by Fred Valentine, who then sold it to Rudolph and Mary (McKay) Hillenkamp.

Isabel and Anna Hillenkamp, two of their children, resided in this home until 1955.

Today, this property boasts Plank Road Pizza, voted best Pizza in St. Charles County

5314 4th Street (1849) Cottleville Wine Seller
Picture from the City of Cottleville
Architectural/Resource Survey (2008)

The building sits on property originally owned by the Cottle family and then by David K. Pitman. In 1849, William H. Luckett bought the land for $12.50 and built a home. William C. Ellis and his wife Elize bought it in January of 1850 for $112.00, then sold the home to James A. Barnes for $450.00. During the Civil War, the home was sold to Herman Pohl for only $275. F. Weinerbur bought the home in 1880 and then Henry Fryer built the current standing structure in 1885. Fryer then sold it to Michael Pfaff. Robert Benson owned the property in 1993, but today it houses the Cottleville Wine Seller, a popular wine garden and restaurant located in Historic Old Town.

5541 Chestnut Street (One room portion built c. 1850)
Picture by Sheryl Guffey (2010)

This original home had a kitchen on the first floor and a sleeping area on the second level. Another two story addition was added in 1915 and a new east side and long front with upstairs dormers expanded the home in 1940. Tom and Lynn Nestor bought the home in 1989 and completed another 1.5 story addition. "The trusses in the original house are natural tree limbs with the bark still on them and the ceiling beams were hand cut with an axe. This part of the house sits on a stacked stone and dirt foundation and with a basement accessible by a cellar door." Tom Nester, from "If Walls Could Talk," *Cottleville Community News*. The hand-cut wood granary on the property appears to have been built in the 1850s. This building was also used as a feed store after the turn of the 20th century. Today, this property houses the unique retail shop called, Blooming Daisy and is owned by the Brewer family.

5350 Main
Picture by Sheryl Guffey (2010) from 4th Street

This building was the Post Office for Cottleville in 1850.

5221 Oak Street General Store and Hotel (1862)
Picture by Sheryl Guffey (2010)

This building was historically used as a general store (Clyde Tiedemann's), with the post office located on the first level in the early 1900s. Hank Keneman resided in this building prior to 1969. This structure mainly remains intact from its original construction and is currently called the Cottleville Antiques-Junk Store.

5366 Main Street (1872) Bross Brothers Home

Today, the home exists over the original stone foundation.

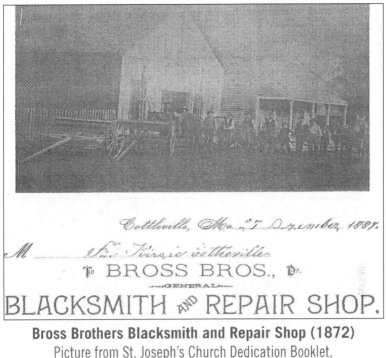

Bross Brothers Blacksmith and Repair Shop (1872)
Picture from St. Joseph's Church Dedication Booklet,
September 16, 1962

The Bross Brothers ran a blacksmith shop at the
corner of Lime and Main Street, next door to their home,
in 1880. This structure no longer remains.

Bross Brothers Blacksmith Shop
Location-Lime and Main (1880)

St. Charles Street (1880-1890) Albert Busch Estate
Sheryl Guffey (2011)

This property now belongs to Frank Martin. Mr. Martin was born and raised on this property.

Frank Martin Picture taken by Sheryl Guffey (2011)

5315 5th Street (1885)

This property was originally owned by the Cottles and then by David K. Pitman. By 1900, it was owned by H. H. Sherman and then sold to George Kohlepp, who was a German cabinet maker and carpenter and the builder of this residence. It was also owned by Henry Hoffman, who was an election judge; thus, voting was held in this location.

5520 St. Charles Street (1885) Lance Law Firm
Picture by Sheryl Guffey

This building was constructed by Gustav Herman.

Dr. J. C Edwards Home (ca. 1885)
Picture at St. Charles County Historical Society

This home no longer remains.

5369 4ᵗʰ Street/ Highway N (ca. 1885)

Dr. Baltzer used this brick building home as his office. After many years, he built a new home and used the side building as his office.

5210 4th Street-Hwy N (1885)

5525 Oak Street (1890-1896) Cottleville Cookies and Cream
Picture by Sheryl Guffey (2011)

This home was built by George Fuhs and had an original entrance on the south elevation. Today, the building houses Cookies and Cream, a favorite place of locals.

Dr. Baltzer Home 5337 4ᵗʰ Street (1892)
Picture from St. Charles County Historic
Society Archives taken in 1927

Michele Hitt Home
Picture by Sheryl Guffey (2011)

Dr. J.C. Edwards built a building for his physician's office at this location around 1885. Dr. M.L. Currier, also a doctor, improved the property around 1905.

The original building was built in 1892 in the Late Victorian style by Dr. Baltzer, who was the son of Adolph Baltzer—the Evangelical Friedens Church minister—and Louisa Van Laer. Dr. Baltzer and Eva Baltzer (Hartman) resided there and had his examination room in a building next to the home (still standing). The Tiedemann family then owned the property and the Bergen family rehabilitated the home. One of Cottleville's earliest residential buildings, it was built in the late Victorian architectural style with intact Colonial Revival detailing. Tax records show that the building was most likely constructed by Casper Landhold.

5291 5th Street (1895)
Picture from the City of Cottleville
Architectural/Historic Resource Survey (2008)

The original lot was owned by David K. Pitman and sold to John Rupp, a German road developer, in 1880. The property was owned by Amanda Hillenkamp however the home no longer exists..

5209 Highway N (1896)
Picture from St. Joseph's Church Dedication Booklet,
September 16, 1962

This building was constructed by German wagon maker Phillip Fischer. It became a home and then the Jeager family operated a general store from it. This building was also the Hillenkamp General Store until 1909. Following their ownership, the Schulte brothers ran a grocery store there, and they lived upstairs. Harold Schneider's family operated a grocery store, gas station, and post office. The building was also once used as apartments, a pizza shop, and a dog grooming salon.

As a teenager, I remember seeing the local farmers sitting on the concrete stoop discussing important issues of the day.

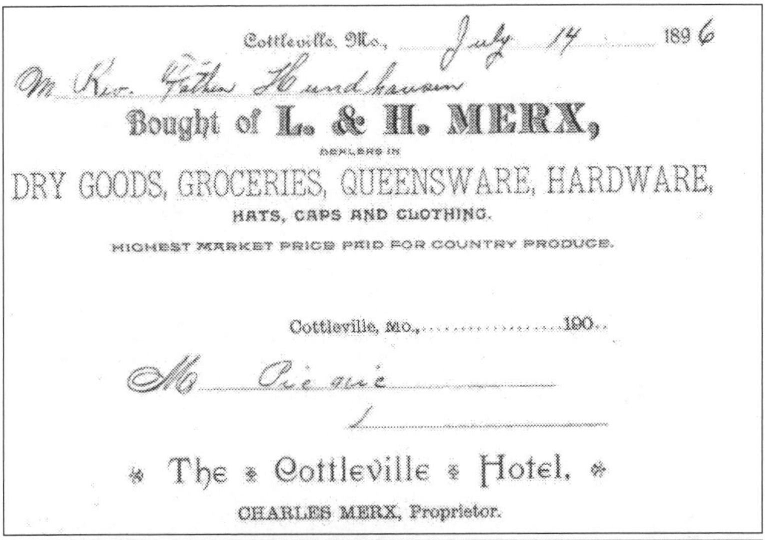

Cottleville, Mo., July 14 1896

M Rev. Father Hundhausen

Bought of L. & H. MERX,

DEALERS IN

DRY GOODS, GROCERIES, QUEENSWARE, HARDWARE,

HATS, CAPS AND CLOTHING.

HIGHEST MARKET PRICE PAID FOR COUNTRY PRODUCE.

Cottleville, Mo.,..................190..

M Picnic

1

The Cottleville Hotel,

CHARLES MERX, Proprietor.

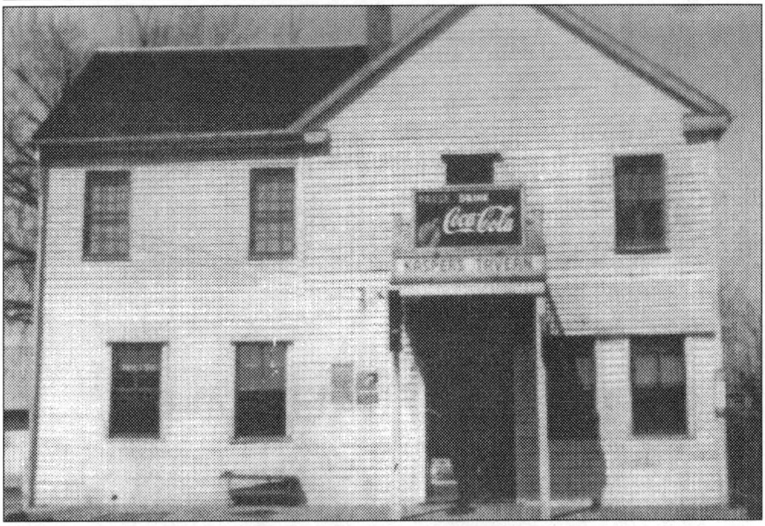

Originally Merx's Hotel 4th Street, Kasper's Tavern and then Clara Lindemann's Tavern

Picture at the St. Charles County Historical Society

The tavern had a two-barrel stove and a signature bar that has been stored for preservation.

Phillip and Mary (Schneider) Vierling Home (ca. 1900s)
Picture from St. Joseph's Church Dedication Booklet,
September 16, 1962

Many Vierling family members rented space within the home. The Vierlings sold it to George and Frieda Kapeller. The building was later sold to the Dickherber family. It burned to the ground and no longer remains.

5206 Gutermuth Road Sigmund Kessler/Lauer Home (1918)

Sigmund Kessler bought property at Motherhead and Gutermuth in 1892 and then the Laer (Virgil – now deceased and Ruth) family owned the property.

Ruth Laer
Picture taken by Sheryl Guffey (2011)

The African Church and their school were located across the road from the Laer home on what is today the play yard at St. Joseph Catholic Church. Mary Crawford now resides in the home.

Chapter 9

Cottleville 1900-1960

The 1905 map of Cottleville shows four churches: Southern Methodist, German Evangelical, African, and Catholic. This map also shows two hotels located at Oak Street and 4th Street, a post office on Oak Street, and two schools: Public School No. 3 on Chestnut Street and the African School on Gutermuth Road.

1905 Cottleville Town Map (shows Cottle Original Town— The David Pitman First Addition and the David Pitman Second Addition donated by David K. Pitman)

St. Charles County Historical Society Archives Cottleville was a growing town. Some resident families of the time were: Sigmund Kessler; Edward Seymour; Rebecca Gillette; Taylor Reed Est, Isam Taggart, M. Jones, Issac Taggart—African-American;, Henry Pieper; John Toelle, Sr.; Amanda Hillenkamp; Cathy Landwehmeier; M. Henning;, George Kohlepp; Frank Feilner; the Bross

Brothers; Peter Iffrig; Herman Baltzer; Henry Rueffer; Daniel Stephens; August Thoene; Daniel Sammelman; Rudolph Hillenkamp; Henry Wolf; William Wolf; Francis Menne; Mary Cordes; Joseph Zerr; Michael Pfaff; Pauline Kappeller; Herman Range; George Fuhs; J. C. Edwards; M.L. Currier; Ed Nienhueser; Ora Cottle; John Pitman; Henry Fardicke; John Gutermuth; Adam and John Arras; Phillip Vierling; Shade and Isabella Kasper; John Schneider; James and Clara Lindemann; Simons; Kessler; D. Stephens; John Hoffmann, Jr.; John D. Sandfort; Auckley Brother; Rosa Hofman; Georg Hoffman; W. F. Gilette; Casanda Auckley; Frank Fehr; Ben Sauer; J.C. Roth; Tiedemann; John Heisel; Jane Heisel; Mrs. Henry Pfeiffer; John Green; John Hoffmann; Boetter; John B; M. L. Currier; Wendell Sammelmann; Jane Voegtle; W. Hunter; John Brueggmann; Herman Pohl; William Hoffmann; John Pfeffer; Otto Deberthauser; Charles Kessler; Daniel Stephens; Henry and Lillian Gutermuth.

On January 25, 1908, local citizens created the Cottleville Fire Department. A 75 cent fee per person was levied to raise funds for the initial operating budget. Only persons that paid this fee were protected by the fire department. The fire department's original coverage was determined by how far the firefighters could pull the hand-drawn equipment from their fire station. The first year's budget was $152.50 and Mr. C. T. Arrons was the first volunteer Fire chief.

Cottleville Volunteer Fire Department 1943 Bud Wilcox, who later became the first part-time Fire chief, is standing on the ground, in the center of the wagon, third from the right. Picture from St. Joseph's Church Dedication Booklet, September 16, 1962

The first station was built on reserved public use property set up by Lorenzo Cottle at the corner of Hwy N and Motherhead Road and is the site of the current Cottleville Fire Department. The fire department was an all-volunteer force that raised additional monies through dances, picnics, bake sales, etc.

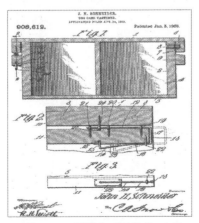

United States Patent #908, 612 Egg-Case Fastener
Image from the United States Patent Office (1909)

John H. Schneider of Cottleville applied for the Egg-Case Fastener on August 14, 1908 and this was patented on January 5, 1909.

Grabau Family Cottleville (1913)
Picture of the home of Edward Nienhueser (volunteer fireman) and Maria Adelheid Nienhueser (Grabau), Pitman's 2nd Addition, Block 3. Picture donated by Judith Kuhl (Schultheis)——descendent of Rev. Carl Frederich, Henry and Elise (Auguste) Hessler, and William Schultheis and Adelaide Margaret (Hessler) Schultheis; and by Karen Conley——, descendent of the Grabau-Hessler families.

Wedding Day (June 18, 1913)
From right: M. Gertrud Mary Whittich, John Henry Friedrich (brother to Maria Adelheid), Maria Adelheid (Grabau) Nienhueser, Edward Nienhueser, Elise Marie Bonnert, unknown. Picture shared by Judith Kuhl and Karen Conley.

Nienhueser Home   **Nienhueser Property**
Pictures shared by Judith Kuhl (2011)

The citizens of Cottleville pursued a drainage district to re-channel the Dardenne Creek to take the winding waters more under control by straightening out the waterway during the 1920s. St. Charles County approved the three miles of ditch work along the

Dardenne Creek in 1930. Some long time residents believe the $4 per acre imposed tax to cover the cost of this project was severe and many lost their property. The final outcome was 14 square miles of drier land that was previously under water for several months every year. The bridge at St. Charles Street, as well as most of Water Street, was no longer constantly under water. Today you can still see where the concrete bridges were built; however, the strength of the water washed away their structures, leaving only remnants of the bridge.

Dredging the Dardenne Creek before more modern equipment was used (ca. 1920s)
Picture shared by Judith Kuhl

Hayford Bridge Collapse over the Dardenne

Picture from *In His Own Hand: A Historical Scrapbook of St. Charles County, Missouri* by John J. Buse (1998)

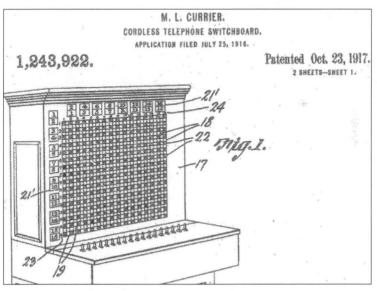

**M.L. Currier of Cottleville Patient
for the Cordless Telephone Switchboard**

Image from the United States Patent Office (1917)

Cottleville had a private benefactor whose 15-page detailed will provided for the beautification of Cottleville. The benefactor was Mr. George F. Miller, who grew up on the Miller farm, which—according to an old plat—abutted the corporate limits of Cottleville. Mr. Miller died in 1921. His $1,000 endowment fund was to provide for maintaining several churches and institutions, including Cottleville and Wolf Cemetery, and a burial ground just outside of Cottleville (Cottle Burying Ground). It also stated that he wanted heart maple shade trees planted and a drinking fountain built. At one time, the money produced one-half of one percent interest, so the money lay dormant for some time. Allan Arras, trustee of Miller's will, saw $160.30 per year of spendable interest and had directed the money to be used for paying Cottleville's street lights.

Cottleville went through hard times after the stock market crash of 1929 and the Great Depression of the 1930s. Cottleville saw very little growth for a decade. Alternative routes west, left the Boones Lick Road only a local thoroughfare that only a few needed and the closing of the Cottle mill meant that the bridge at St. Charles Street led only to farm land.

5344 4th Street-Hwy N (1932)

MAKING UP for "Uncle Ephraim's Summer Boarders," at Union School, Cottleville, coached by Miss Marie Brink — Bernice Wiechens, Isabel Wiechens, Miss Brink, Anna Ohmes, Marjorie Henry, Sophia Schumann, Lavelle Rieffer, Loyola Auckly, Lucille Ohmes, Margaret Auberschaum, Alvina Wehmeier, Myrtle Rieffer, Olga Schumann. At right, Wilbert Wiechens, Ray Rieffer, Robert Gerdts, Rolla Henry, Earl Rieffer, Ernest Gerdts, Albert Rieffer, Emil Ohmes, Othmar Auckly.

St. Louis Post-Dispatch, June 14, 1936
Union School was located north of Cottleville
along present-day Birdie Hills Road.

Mr. William Stoll 1940 Picture from St. Joseph's Church
Dedication Booklet, September 16, 1962

It is claimed by many that Mr. Stoll was the last
resident to have used his horse and buggy. In the 1940s,
Highway N was paved through Cottleville following the
old Booneslick Road into town and headed north out of
the city along Fourth Street.

The United States government constructed a TNT
plant in Weldon Spring, Missouri (about 3.5 miles from
Cottleville) in 1940. This plant displaced many from their
homes and leveled the township of Hamburg. Father
Pezold and many citizens created the Village of All Saints
consisting of 24 homes, mainly constructed from building
materials torn down from the TNT plant site. Cottleville
increased in population from 1940 to 1950, but still
remained small.

The Cottleville Fire Department sold subscription tags for one dollar each and they bought a 1931 Ford Model A pumper. Many community events took place at the fire hall.

Cottleville Baseball Team, 1948 Picture from St. Joseph's Church Dedication Booklet, September 16, 1962

Townspeople remember the great flood through the Dardenne Creek bottoms in 1952. Many could only travel by boat if they wished to go west of Cottleville. I saw pictures of residents in boats, fishing, but for the most part, it was dangerous and restricting. In December 2015, there was another flood of the bottoms, larger than in 1952.

I met with Lucille Kasper (Fetch) at her home in Cottleville in May of 2011. She moved to Cottleville in 1938 and married Russell Kasper, whose father created Kasper's Tavern. Lucille was delightful in her recollections of past years in Cottleville, describing the people and activities of the day and remembered Cottleville with only gravel roads. Lucille stories are indicative of the pride and quaintness of so many people who have lived their lives in Cottleville.

5339 5ᵗʰ Street (1950)

The Kasper family lived in this house.

Buggy in front of Kasper's Tavern
Picture at the St. Charles Historical Society

Shade Kasper, in his later years, sold his Tavern to James Lindemann on the morning of June 4, 1957. Mr. Lindemann was found dead that afternoon on his farm, but Clara Lindemann continued with the contract and ran the tavern for many years.

Clara's Tavern
Picture owned by James Lindemann

Many in Cottleville remember the red bud tree in front of Clara's Tavern, and her 50 cent Catfish Platter.

5335 Hwy N - Oak Street (1954) Meridith Struebing Photography-In the Moment-A Family Affair
Picture by Sheryl Guffey (2011)

The Schulte family rented this home to many Cottleville residents over the years. The Schulte family owned a well company and sold water and delivered it to area cisterns around Cottleville. There are those who still remember the Schulte cattle drives that went through the center of town. The Bruce family lived at 5335 Hwy N (Cottleville Crafts Etc... today) and rented part of the property for a below ground mechanic and lawn repair shop. Charles and Marlene Schlueter live next door. This quaint shop is now owned by Sheryl Guffey in the Historic District of Cottleville. I am especially proud to have a place of business in the original Cottleville township (Block 4-Lot 4) laid out by Lorenzo Cottle, my relative, at the corner of 5th and Oak in the Old Town Historic District.

Frank and Helen Wies are a legend in Cottleville, having had 11 children, 52 grandchildren, 85 great grandchildren and 8 great-great grandchildren. Helen was born in Cottleville in 1908 to Robert and Aldina Pfaff and grew up in the house across the street from Frank Ochs. Adlina lived to be 94 years old. "I remember my friends and I used to love to watch the blacksmith at work, sharpening the blades for the plows." Helen Wies, *Cottleville Call*, Vol.4, No.3. Weiss Road, which bordered the Weis property, was named after the family, but the road sign was misspelled.

Helen Weis Picture from *Cottleville Call* (2001)

Cottleville was officially incorporated in 1853; however, the city had lain dormant since 1881. In 1953, St. Charles County questioned whether re-incorporation was appropriate. The city's citizens hired an attorney to confirm that, once a village was incorporated, it was always incorporated. The ruling was that Cottleville was still a city. Cottleville celebrated its 100th year since incorporation in 1953.

The Official Manual of the State of Missouri commonly called the Blue Book, published by the Missouri Secretary of State's Office,—listed Cottleville's population at 150 residents in 1964 and 230 residents in 1970. O'Fallon and St. Peters wanted to annex a large area of Cottleville during this time. Things began to change.

Chapter 10

Cottleville Explodes

In 1972, Cottleville elected a Board of Trustees for the first time in 98 years. That year also saw Cottleville start operating as a city with elected officials, including its first mayor, Steve Kochanski. The Cottleville Community Fire Protection District was also created in 1972 from the existing Fire Department. In 1980, Cottleville only had a population of 184; however, the city grew to 453 by 1990. The government became very involved. Eighteen properties on Highway N were incorporated into the city. Cottleville started annexing land, servicing citizens, and began charging taxes.

St. Charles County Community College
Picture by Sheryl Guffey (2011)

St. Charles County Community College was established by the Community College District and built in Cottleville in 1986. The first classes held in the summer of 1987 had 400 students, but enrollment increased to 1,547 by that fall.

Norman "Bud" Wilcox was the first part-time Fire Chief for 30 years. A 10-cent tax election allowed the hiring of Mark Bodhle as the first full-time firefighter in July of 1982 and the hiring Jim Litteken as the first-full time Fire chief in October of 1982. Doug Kane was then hired as a full-time firefighter and Skip Gauldin was hired as a full-time Training Officer in 1986.

Cottleville Fire Protection District's (CFPD) "Headquarters" Station Dedication Ceremony (1987)

CFPD picture by Sheryl Guffey (2011)

The Cottleville Fire Protection Station was built in 1987 for about $850,000. Today, the Cottleville Community Fire Protection District encompasses four fire stations and serves 38 square miles of St. Charles County, responding to over 2,600 calls per year.

There has been a long-time interest from Cottleville residents to establish a Cottleville Historical District. The Cottleville Historical Committee was organized in August of 1989, with its main purpose to establish rules and regulations for the historical district and submit them to the trustees to pass and enforce. "Our main concern is controlling and preserving the old buildings. We need some sort of governing power to stop the destruction of the historic buildings and control new construction." Georgette Bergen, Village Trustee and Historical Committee Chairwoman, "History in the Making: Cottleville Residents Seeking to Establish Historical District," *St. Charles Journal*, Dec. 9, 1989. That year also marked the chartering of the Cottleville Kiwanis Club.

St. Peters and O'Fallon were experiencing explosive growth in their populations and were very aggressive in annexations during the early 1990s. Cottleville officials took action and began its own annexation plan. The city became one of the fastest growing communities in the state of Missouri through the 1990s. The Highway 370 Discovery Bridge over the Missouri River, which connects St. Louis to St. Charles County, was opened to traffic in 1992. Cottleville sits in the center of an area called "The Golden Triangle"—a triangular intersection of three major highways: Interstate 70, Interstate 64, and Highway 94. Many Cottleville residents decided to protect its boundaries and the dormant little town sprang into action. Cottleville had been organized under the leadership of a Board of Trustees until it elected a new mayor, Stephen Kochanski, and elected Alderman. Cottleville became a fourth-class city on August 4, 1992. The first police department and court was established that same year.

Important Cottleville elected and paid leaders included: Stephen Kochanski, Bob Powers, Sandy Barklage, Amy Spencer, Scott Lewis, Mike Underwood, Don Buchheit, Mark Holquin, Wayne Litwiller, Matt

Jacobs, Barbara Mitchell, Tim Pemberton, Jennifer Wagner, Sally Faith, Serall Chezem, Ron Walter, Pat McEvoy, Jennifer Wagner, Joel Young, Michael Sommers, and Paul Lorton. The St. Charles Journal's December 10, 1995 issue reported that the Board of Alderman has approved an ordinance rezoning a 75-acre tract of land known as the Schneider tract. This ordinance allowed for 202 homes just off of Weis Road. The developer, Harold Burkemper, gave the city $100,000 to offset costs arising from the increased population density at a time when Cottleville's yearly revenue was about $220,000.

Vantage Park Lake
Picture taken by Sheryl
Guffey (2009)

Named after the company that constructed Madison Park subdivision, Vantage Homes dedicated 23 acres to the City of Cottleville to create Vantage Park. Vantage Park features a 9-acre lake and a 0.7- mile walking trail. The lake is stocked with catfish and small mouth bass, and hosts an annual fishing derby.

The Office of Missouri State Auditor Claire McCaskill discovered some problems concerning closed meetings and an interest- free loan agreement that the city entered into without voter approval during the years 1996-1998. Cottleville government operated out of as many as 36 places, until it organized into a temporary building at

1280 Motherhead Road in 1999. All matters were resolved with having a city governmental site and structure.

The U.S. Census from the year 2000 reported that Cottleville's population was 1,929, which illustrated a growth rate of more than 300 percent from 1990. Organizations were formed, the Knights of Columbus Father William Pezold Council #7198, which built a new building at 5701 Highway N. Cottleville elected its next mayor, Bob Powers, and the *Cottleville Call*, a resource newsletter for the residents of Cottleville, was created.

The City of Cottleville needed to increase its sales tax revenue. Cottleville administrators talked with trustees of two area subdivisions, The Meadows of Manor Lake and Dardenne Farms, as well as the developer Westbound Investments, LLC,. to form a 484–acre commercial rezoning plan in 2001. The 41 acres between Highway N on the north and Dardenne Creek on the south was zoned as a Planned Unit Development, allowing city officials to control what businesses would be allowed. A buffer zone was established to make commercial development be at least 100 feet away from property lines. C-3 commercial zoning was established encompassing 65 acres between Dardenne Creek on the north and Crooked Creek on the south. Cottleville zoned 216 acres of flood plain to be developed at Westbound's cost, for city parks. To create the parks, one million cubic yards of dirt was to be moved from the flood plain to Highway 94 and Mid Rivers Mall Drive for the cloverleaf of the Page Avenue extension (Hwy 364). In 2018, Cottleville will have an on and off ramp to Hwy 364 on Gutermuth Road.

City of Cottleville Zoning Map
The population of Cottleville was 2,059 in 2003—Cottleville's sesquicentennial year.

Warren Elementary School
Picture by Sheryl Guffey (2011)
Warren Elementary, named in honor of Warren Cottle, was built and opened for the 2000-2001 school year.

In 2002, the Cottleville-Weldon Spring Chamber of Commerce was formed.

Students in the St. Joseph 75ᵗʰ Anniversary of Parade
Picture from Cottleville News (2006)

By 2006, the City of Cottleville had grown to 2,596 and in 2009 the U.S. Census Department reported that Cottleville had a population of 3,227. The medium resident age of Cottleville in 2010 was 38.2 years, with a medium household income of $89,320. Missouri had a medium household income of only $45,229. In 2009, Cottleville residents owned homes or condominiums at a medium value of $280,537, while the Missouri medium was only $139,700.

**Cottleville Weldon Spring Rotary Club
Amazing Race 2007 1ˢᵗ Place Team**
Lindsay Jones, Nick Jones, Amy Spencer,
Scott Lewis, Jay Diekmann, Tracy Diekmann
Picture from *Cottleville News* 2007

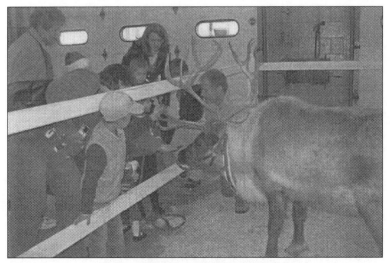

Christmas in Cottleville 2007
Picture from *Cottleville Community News* First Quarter (2007)

Cottleville City Hall and Police Department 5490 Fifth Street Picture taken by Sheryl Guffey (2010)

The Cottleville City Hall and Police Department is one of the first green Leadership in Energy and Environmental Design (LEED) designed buildings in St. Charles County and cost $5.3 million to build. It sits on a 40-acre site on Route N at the northern edge of Old Town and comprises 15,888 square feet of space designed by Kostecki Architects. A ribbon cutting ceremony was held on February 28, 2009. The welcome speech was made by City Administrator and Police Chief Scott Lewis, with the invocation by Pastor Daniel Perrin of Grace Presbyterian Church, and speeches by Rex M. Burlison (Regional Director for Missouri Governor Jay Nixon) and Mayor Don Yarber. The benediction was given by David Rispoli of Joy Community Church.

Don Yarber - Former Mayor of Cottleville
Picture by Sheryl Guffey (2010)

In January of 2010, the Board of Aldermen unanimously passed a resolution urging state leaders to move forward with medical marijuana legislation allowing marijuana use for medical purposes. Mayor Don Yarber pressed for a state-wide ballot initiative; however, the citizens of Cottleville defeated the initiative that April.

Cottleville is one of 50 Missouri communities that are certified by the U.S. Department of the Interior's National Park Service and the Missouri Department of Natural Resources' State Historic Preservation Office as a Certified Local Government. This certification is intended to encourage preservation of the community's historic structures. The streetscape pedestrian system connects City Hall to the internal trail system of Legacy City Park.

Legacy Park Cabin

Legacy Park Playground Equipment
Pictures taken by Sheryl Guffey (2000)

Legacy Park is a 37-acre park hosting football and soccer fields, a softball field, children's playground equipment, a dog park, and a four multi-purpose shelters for family use. A spacious amphitheater for cultural and performance attractions is located within Legacy Park. The park has one of two Missouri Devine Liberty

Swings. The Liberty Swing allows wheelchair bound children to go to the park and enjoy their own swing. The Swing Grand Opening was held on June 5, 2011. The playground is designed for ages 2-12. Purchase of this Swing was made possible by dedicated fundraising activities of the Cottleville Firefighters Community Outreach organization the Liberty Swing Committee and many local businesses. The total cost of the project was approximately $60,000.

Divine Liberty Swing Picture from *Community News* (May 18, 2011)

CFO (Cottleville Firefighters Outreach) Members with Francis Howell Children (2011)

Cottleville Firefighters Outreach, a 501(c)(3) charitable organization, was established in 2009 to assist those in need and holds an annual St. Patrick's Day fundraising event in Cottleville. The event usually brings about 25,000 people to Cottleville to participate in the "Run for the Helmet" walk/run race and parade.

In 2016, Kochanski Sports Field was constructed in honor of the late Stephen Kochanski, who served as Cottlevilles' first Mayor.

Bark Park features two sections; a large one acre area for large dogs and another section for small breeds. Within the park, is also sand volleyball courts, basketball hoops, tennis courts and old log cabin.

Cottle ville is part of the Dardenne Greenway Multi-use Trail System and offers a place to walk, run, bicycle, rollerblade or to take a golf cart ride. The Koontz Fort Trail, completed in 2015 is also another trail in Cottleville lined by woods and follows the old Boones Lick Trail.

Vantage Lake, in Cottleville, is a nine acre lake accessible via a 10' wide pedestrian bridge over the Dardenne Creek. Vantage Lake has a small gazebo, a restroom and offers a 7 mile paved walking trail. Many people have utilized the Community Garden near Vantage Lake.

Harmony Lake, located near the St. Charles Community College is a five acre lake with a fishing dock, pavillions and a 6 mile paved walking trail. Harmony Lake got its name from the former property owner, Mrs. Poahorn who always said she enjoyed the peace and harmony of her farm.

Chapter 11

Cottleville Streetscape

Historic Old Town Cottleville preserves the small town charm of the past while providing a streetscape for residents and visitors. We can enjoy walking, shopping, and dining while taking in the natural and historic beauty of this quaint community. The Streetscape Project produced wide sidewalks that emulate the historic Boone's Lick wooden plank road that once connected St. Charles and Cottleville, historic street lights, and landscaping that lines the corridor. The Streetscape Project's construction phase Dedication Ceremony was held on March 3, 2011.

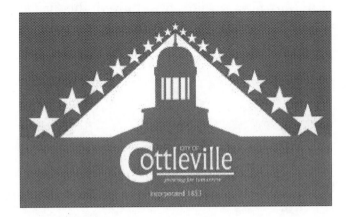

"Lighting will be reminiscent of old-fashioned square lantern-style fixtures, with black wrought iron fluted poles. The sidewalks will be of stamped concrete to resemble wood planks, replicating the old Western Plank Road that ran from St. Charles to Cottleville in the 1880s." then City Administrator Scott Lewis, presently St. Charles County Sheriff.

Cottleville at Hwy N (2011) Pictures taken by Sheryl Guffey

Earth Angel - Canvas and Cocktails

Bemos
Pictures taken by Sheryl Guffey (2010)

Mannino's Meat Market

Jo's 5th Street Pub
Pictures taken by Sheryl Guffey (2011)

Cottleville is a golf cart community that allows access throughout town to local shopping centers and its parks. Visitors and residents can take a stroll through town, enjoying eateries, a local meat market, a wine garden and specialty shops, while enjoying the historic buildings and local history.

Mayor Jim Hennessey from 2013 to present

RANKED 6ᵀᴴ NATIONALLY IN POPULATION GROWTH BY PERCENTAGE
United States Census Bureau

Cottleville Banner. Old Town Cottleville
Picture by Sheryl Guffey (2010)

Cottleville is home to the Francis Howell Central High School Spartans, Louis C. Saeger Middle School Spartans, Warren Elementary School, and St. Joseph Catholic Grade School. Cottleville also has St. Charles Community College, a two-year college, established in 1986. SCC is now the fourth largest of Missouri's 12 Community College districts with 11,629 students in 2017. President Dr. Barbara Kavalier oversees the 95 full-time academic staff and the 324 full-time administrative staff.

College Meadows Park has become St. Charles County's 11th regional park. Located in Cottleville, on the campus of St. Charles Community College. College Meadows Park encompasses 80 acres with a fitness trail and a nine-hole frisbee golf course.

Cottleville also is home to Hansen Park located behind Mercy Medical. Hansen Park was named in honor of Jeff Hansen who was a major contributor to area charities. McAuley Playground Hansen Park, is an all inclusive playground specifically designed to remove physical and social barriers so all children with or without disabilities and/or critical illnesses can play side by side. McAuley Playround is named in honor of Sister Catherine McAuley who founded the Sisters of Mercy Health.

Chapter 12

A Bright Future Ahead

Scott A. Lewis Park is the newest addition to the Cottleville Park System. This 65 acre park has two lakes totaling 25 acres. Buccheit Lake has a boat ramp for electric motor boat launching and a 8'wide paved trail. Bucheit Lake is named after Don Buchheit who served Cottleville for more than 30 years as Alderman in Ward 2.Scott A. Lewis Park has a large pavillion for 60 guests and is named after Cottlevilles Chief of Police/City Administrator and currently St. Charles Co. Sherif.

Cottleville was ranked 6th nationally in population growth by percentage in 2016.

Sunset in Cottleville along Gutermuth Road
Picture by Sheryl Guffey (2011)

Cottleville has ebbed and flowed like the waterways that surround its boundaries, but is undeniably in a growth phase that will continue. Growth came when paved roads led to Cottleville and many more will join our community as new interconnecting Missouri highways pass through our boundaries. Highway 364 (Page Avenue Extension) has create easy access to St. Louis County and Highway 94 redevelopment has eased travel through St. Charles County. Cottleville is a growing, dynamic city that reflects the enthusiasm of its young people, the vitality of its families, and the wisdom of its seniors. Cottleville is also a community that cherishes tradition and values, while embracing an optimistic vision of the future.

Lafser and Associates identified one site in Cottleville which qualifies for the local and National Registry; the Cottle Mill.

Fourteen additional sites have been identified as possible listings. Up to a total 37 properties were identified, some becoming eligible with proper materials being restored.

Careful consideration for our heritage must be in the forefront of future plans. The promise of Cottleville lies in its local people, city administrators, land developers, and future generations. The Cottleville Historic Commission will need to continue to serve us well in the preservation, restoration and renovation of Historic Cottleville. Modern conveniences accompanied by our quaint historic heritage will continue to create a unique environment for all to enjoy. Our proud past reaches up to the present and lets us remember that Cottleville is where history never grows old.

Remnants of the past Picture taken by Sheryl Guffey (2010)

This equipment, an old hay bailer and seeder quietly resting under some of Cottleville's native hickory groves, is reminiscent of farm work of days gone by.

End Notes

1. Joseph Harl, Dennis Naglich, and John Fulmer *Master Plan for the Management of Archeological Resources within St. Charles County*: (Missouri: Archaeological Research Center of St. Louis, Missouri, 1997), p.1.

2. Ibid, p.52, ASM Site #23SC62.

3. Ibid, p.55, ASM Site #23SC68, 23SC497, 23CS67, and 23SC507.

4. Ibid, p. 65, ASM Sites #23SC507, #23SC699, #23SC701, #23SC822/825, and #23SC926.

5. Ibid, p.107, Site #23SC55/66 Distribution Center.

6. Ibid, p. 144, ASM Sites #23SC and #822/825.

7. Paul C. Nagel, *The Later Letters of Ralph Waldo Emerson 1843-1871*: (Lawrence: University Press of Kansas, 1977).

8. Aubrey Hoare, *The History of Wilts* Volume IV and V., pp. 117-118.

9.   W. H. Cottell, *A History of the Cotel, Cottell, or Cottle Family of the Counties of Devon, Somerset, Cornwall and Wilts* (England: Taylor & Company, 1871).

10.   Poole, *New Vineyard*, The quotations are edited from the Hough's Forward and Chapter I, pp.8-16.

11.   Mary Grace Canfield, *The Valley of the Kedron: The Story of the South Parish, Woodstock, Vermont* pp. 287-88, as quoted in Music, *Cottle Genealogy*, p. 15.

12.   Kemp Dixon, *From Plymouth Rock to Rocky Creek*: (Austin, Texas: Morgan Printing, 2008), p. 33.

13.   Henry Dana Swan, *History of Woodstock, Vermont*: (Boston & New York: Houghton, Mifflin & Company, 1889), p.53.

14.   *Vermont Revolutionary Rolls*, p. 280.

15.   Velma Cottle Musick, *The Cottle Genealogy*: (Kingfisher, Oklahoma: privately published, 1965), pp.15-16.

Sources

Stephen Ambrose, *Undaunted Courage: Meriwether Lewis, Thomas Jefferson, and the Opening of the American West*: (New York: Simon & Shuster, 1996).

William Fletcher Barnds, (1840-1926), Papers, 1900s-1920s.

Charles Banks, Dr., *The History of Martha's Vineyard, Volume III Family Genealogies*: The Cottle Family c.1925, pp.106-115.

Daniel Brown, Dr., *Small Glories: A Memoir of Southern St. Charles County and the Formation of the Francis Howell School District*: (St. Louis: Independent Publishing Corporation, 2003).

John J. Buse, *In His Own Hand: A Historical Scrapbook of St. Charles County, Missouri*, (1998).

Byran & Rose, eds. *A History of the Pioneer Families of Missouri: St. Charles, Montgomery and Warren County* (St. Louis: Brand & Co., 1876).

Frederic Billion, *Annals of St. Louis in its Territorial Days, from 1804 to 1821*: (St. Louis: Frederic L. Billon, 1888).

Mary Grace Canfield, *The Valley of the Kendron*: (South Woodstock, Vermont: Kedron Associates, 1940).

Clarence Edwin Carter, *Territorial Paper of the United States*: (Buffalo, New York: W. S. Hein, 1934).

Carl H.Chapman, *The Archaeology of Missouri, I*: (Columbia: University of Missouri Press, 1975).

Earl A. Collins, *"The Multitudes Incorporated"* (Missouri Historical Review, Vol. XVIII, No. 4, July, 1933), pp. 308-309.

Reverend John Collinson, *"The History and Antiquities of the County of Somerset"* (Bath: R. Crittwell, 1791), Vol.111, p.330.

Henry E. Cottle, *"Cottle Family (Edward Cottle, ca. 1628-1710)*: (Bristol- Reynolds Historical Genealogy Report: Connecticut).

W. H. Cottell, member of the Harleian Society, Etc. *A History of the Cotel, Cottell, or Cottle Family of the Counties of Devon, Somerset, Cornwall and Wilts*: (England: Taylor and Co., Little Queen Street Lincoln's Inn Fields, 1871).

William Foley, *Genesis of Missouri: From Wilderness Outpost To Statehood*: (1989).

Henry Swan Dana, *The History of Woodstock, Vermont*: (Boston: Houghton Mifflin, 1889).

Kemp Dixon, *From Plymouth Rock to Rocky Creek*: (Austin, Texas: Morgan Printing, 2008).

David Wolf Eaton, *How Missouri Counties, Towns and Streams Were Named*: (Columbia, Missouri: The State Historical Society of Missouri, 1916). Article written in 1884. Transcribed from "The Missouri Historical Review," Vol. XVIII, No. 1, October 1, 1918.

Steve Ehlmann, *Crossroads: A History of St. Charles County, Missouri*: (Marceline, Missouri: Walsworth Publishing Company, 2004).

William E. Foley, *A History of Missouri Vol. 1, 1683-1820*: (Columbia: University of Missouri Press, 1971).

Dan Haas and Roger Boyd, *An Archaeological Survey of Sample Transects in the Lower Missouri River Basin* (Privately published by Reidhead, Chapman, and Haas 1977).

Joseph Harl, Dennis Naglich, and John Fulmer *Volume 1: Master Plan for the Management of Archaeological Resources within St. Charles County, MO* Research Report #51 (1997).

Eugenia L. Harrison, *"Place Names of Four River Counties In Eastern Missouri.* M.A. Thesis, University of Missouri-Columbia, (1943).

Jon L. Hawker, *Missouri Landscapes: A Tour Through Time* (1992).

C. S. Hoppin, *"The Washington Ancestry and Records of the McClain, Johnson, and Forty Other Colonial American Families*: (Privately printed. 1932), Vol. III, pp 437-457, has a chapter on "The Cottles of Wiltshire and Martha's Vineyard."

Oliver Howard, *Census of St. Charles County, Territory of Missouri*, 1817 and 1819, Indexer.

David Hoyt, "*Old Families of Salisbury and Amesbury* by 1897."

Thomas Louis, Editor, *Valley of the Mississippi*: (St. Louis: Hawthorne Publishing Co., 1841).

D.T. Madox, *Late Account of the Missouri Territory*: (St. Charles County Historical Society, 1989).

Perry McCandless, *A History of Missouri, 1820-1860, Volume 11*: (Columbia: University of Missouri Press, 1971).

Velma Cottle Musick, *The Cottle Genealogy, A History of the Cottles in America from 1638*: (Kingsfisher, Oklahoma: privately published 1961 and 1965).

Paul C. Nagel, *Missouri, A History* (Lawrence: University Press of Kansas, 1977), *The Later Letters of Ralph Waldo Emerson*, 1843-1871, p. 50.

D.W.C. Packard, *Celebration of the Two-Hundredth Anniversary of the Incorporation of Bridgewater, Massachusetts, at West Bridgewater, June 3, 1856*: (Boston: J. Wilson and Son, 1856).

Yvonne Castens Prough, Darst Bottom: *A History of Darst Bottom in the Femme Osage Region of St. Charles County, Missouri* (Defiance, Missouri, privately published 2001).

Perry S. Rader, *The History of Missouri*: (Jefferson City, Missouri: Hugh Stevens Company, 1817).

James B. Schwabe, Compiler, *The Cottle Family: Ancestors & Descendants of Sylvanus & Abigail (Sherman) Cottle* First Edition: (Decorah, Iowa: The Anundsen Publishing Co., 1987). A collection of 464 pages of materials on the Cottles.

James B. Schwabe, *Ancestors and Descendants of Sylvanus & Abigail (Sherman) Cottle.* Second Edition (Cottage Mills, IL: privately published, 1993).

Jeffrey E. Smith, *Seeking a Newer World: The Fort Osage Journals and Letters of George Sibley 1808-1811* (St. Charles, Missouri: Lindenwood University Press, 2003).

Paul N. Spellman, *Zadock and Minerva Cottle Woods: American Pioneers* (Austin, 1987). A biography based on Spellman's Master's Thesis.

Kenneth. Stamp, *America in 1857, A Nation on the Brink:* (New York: Oxford University Press, 1990).

Venecia V., Laurence R., and Joycelyn H. Spellman, Editors. *A Family Anthology:* (Privately published, 1988). A collection of 502 pages of family writings and genealogical charts.

Donna Walton, *"Switzer's History of Missouri, St. Louis, 1879 Transcription."*

David J. Weber, *The Spanish Frontier in North America:* (New Haven, Connecticut: Yale University Press, 1992).

Henry Whittemore, *"Genealogical Guide to the Early Settlers of America,"* p. 115.

Kristie C. Wolferman, *The Osage in Missouri*: (Columbia: University of Missouri Press 1997).

Portrait and Biographical Record of St. Charles, Lincoln and Warren Counties: (Chicago: Chapman Publishing Company, 1895).

Newspapers

Cottleville Call, Volume 4, No. 3, 2001.

Lead Belt News (Flat River, Missouri), June 2, 1965.

St. Charles Journal (St. Charles, Missouri), April 16, 1964.

St. Charles Post-Dispatch (St. Charles, Missouri), February 13 and Nov. 29, 1988.

"Traces of Early Indian Village are Found in St. Charles County", *St. Louis Post- Dispatch*, August 12, 1966.

Suburban Journals, St. Charles, Missouri, 2008.

The St. Charles Cosmos, March 6, 1873.

Benjamin Emmons, *Who's Who* 1922-23.

Genealogical Records

Ancestry.com. *Massachusetts Soldiers and Sailors in the War of the Revolution*, 17 Vols. Provo, Utah: The Generations Network, Inc., 1998.

Ancestry.com. *1970 United States Federal Census*. Provo, Utah: The Generations Network, Inc., 2000.

Edmund West, Compiler. *Family Data Collection-Births*. Provo, Utah: The Generations Network, Inc., 2001.

New England Historic Genealogical Society *Massachusetts Town Death Records*. Provo, Utah: The Generations Network, Inc., 1999.

Cemetery List, *Oak* Grove Cemetery *Records*, by F. B. Brockgreitens, City Clerk, City of St. Charles, Missouri.

Online Sources

Ancestry.com
Callaway.county.missouri.org
Missouri Digital Heritage
Missouri Project
Myfamily.com
Rootsweb.com
Usgennet.org
www.stjoecot.org
Missouri Digital Heritage...Education Timeline of Missouri History.

Ancestry.com, *The Cottle Name in History*. Provo, Utah: The Generations Network, 2007.

Miscellaneous

1840 Census.

1860 Census.

1870 Census.

1880 Census;

32nd Annual Report of the Bureau of Labor Statistics State of Missouri. C. Horton, 1910.

Bikeable-Walkable Community Plan. Trailnet, Inc., 2008.

Correspondence from Ben Friberg to author, 2010.

City of Cottleville.

County Atlas, 1875, pp. 12, 14.

French and Spanish Archives, 1763-1841, Folders 1, 2 and 3.

Historical St. Charles, Montgomery and Warren Counties, Missouri, 1985.

National Historical Company (1885), pp. 369 and 453.

"History of Windsor County, VT."

"The Modern Doomsday Book of England."

St. Charles County Historical Society, *Heritage Treasures: An anthology of articles from 20 years of the St. Charles County Heritage* (Published for its 50th Anniversary 1956-2006).

"St. Joseph's Church 1962 Dedication Book."

Township Plats: Road Map of St. Charles County.

Vital Records of Brookfield, Massachusetts, to the end of the year 1949 (Worcester, Massachusetts: Franklin P. Rice, 1909).

Notes

Missouri information:

Missouri's motto in Latin, Salus populi suprema lex esto, means "The welfare of the people shall be the supreme law," Missouri is known as the "Show-Me" State. Our state bird is the bluebird, the state animal is the Missouri mule, the state fish is the channel catfish, the insect is the honeybee, the flower is the White hawthorne blossom, the tree is the flowering dogwood, and our song is the "Missouri Waltz." The first great mastodon found in the world was reconstructed from bones found in Missouri.

Cottle Name

1.　Metonymic occupational name for a cutler, from Old French co(u)tell, co(u)teau 'knife' (Late Latin cutellus, a diminutive of culter 'p[lowshare')
2.　Metonymic occupational name for a maker of chain-mail, from an Anglo-Norman French diminutive of Old French cot(t)e 'coat of mail'. THE COTTLE NAME IN HISTORY, The Generations Network, 2007. Published by The Generations Network, Utah.

Going back to Ancient Egypt, there are traces of the surname COTTA found in Egyptian carvings. The family surname, Cottle, has persisted for centuries, appearing also in the time of the Roman Empire in the Latin form, COTTA. Accuracy in tracing the name begins with the French Norman period of European history. In the French form, the name is COUTELLE. A branch of the family migrating to Germany during the time of Charlemagne set up the name variation COTTSCHALK, which is simply the Germanic form of the present name COTTLE. With the Norman conquest of England in 1066, the French knights of this name went to England. Seen after 1100, the name is recorded in England in the Anglo-French form COTTELL. John Cothulle, born 1277, is an example of the Middle English language period which used the suffix hulle in place of the suffix le. At this time in England, we find the name of Roger Cotel listed on the Hundred Rolls (tax books). "The Modern Doomsday Book of England carries reference to Cottle as being of the old Middle English language period using Cothulle and Cotel."

Captain Warren Cottle

Warren Cottle b. 1755 d. 1811: Revolutionary War Soldier Captain of Vermont Stone and bronze marker
Picture by Sheryl Guffey 2009

St. Charles Daughters of the American Revolution (D.A.R.) sponsored the dedication ceremony and Veterans of Foreign Wars (V.F.W.) Kohl-Jeck Post 2866 assisted and set the tomb stone furnished by the government. The D.A.R. State Regent, Mrs. Clarence Kemper of Clinton, officiated the unveiling at Oak Grove Cemetery. Bernard Cottle of Rowaytown, Connecticut read a biographical sketch prepared by Dr. Eugene Cottle of Laramie, Wyoming. "The great move by Captain Warren Cottle and his family to the Spanish country west of the Mississippi River demonstrates the hardy character and adventurous personality of this man. He doubtless envisioned an expanding nation and once again desired to be on the frontier, the advancing line of settlement. There was a fairly large company of settlers which Captain Cottle led from Vermont to the new land. The fact that this fairly extensive number of people were willing to risk the many hazards of a journey into unknown, unsettled, and foreign country under the supervision of this one man, attests to the qualities of leadership and responsibility which were apparent in the character of Captain Warren Cottle." (*Lead Belt News*, Flat River, St. François County, Missouri, Wed,. June 2, 1965.)

Warren E. Hearnes, Governor of Missouri, sent the following letter to be read at the ceremony:

TO MEMBERS OF THE ST. CHARLES CHAPTER DAUGHTERS OF THE AMERICAN REVOLUTION

I note with great interest your dedication of a Government Revolutionary War marker for Captain Warren Cottle, May 15, Oak Grove Cemetery.

I know the satisfaction which your dedication to the memory of such men as him brings you since I understand this is the first time in thirty years your chapter has found such an unmarked grave. May I offer my congratulations and best wished to the 30 direct descendants, guests from many places, my fellow Missourians and their organizations, including your chapter of the D.A.R, who will attend.

Sincerely,
Warren B. Hearnes

The Cottle, Woods and Spellmann families (Guffey) are direct descendents from **Zadock Woods and Minerva Woods (Cottle).** Zadock Woods (1773-1842) married Minerva Cottle, who was a descendent of Governor William Bradford of the Plymouth Colony and the daughter of Deacon Joseph and Azubah (Power) Cottle. Both Zadock and Minerva were from Woodstock, Vermont. In 1799 Zadock Woods, Jonathan Jr., and Joseph Cottle moved their families to the St. Charles District.

Minerva Woods (Cottle) b. December 22, 1776 d. March 28, 1839 m. Zadock Woods b. September 18, 1773 d. September 18, 1842

Zaddock Woods

Montraville Woods b. November 17, 1806 at Woods
Fort d. July 15, 1857 m. Isabella Gonzales Hidalgo
June 1826 b. July 2, 1812 at Woods Fort

Emma Ardelia Woods (Hartman) b. December 27,
1854(1) at Woods Fort d. November 20, 1939 m.
William Hartman January 27, 1881

Edward Franklin Hartman b. November 7, 1893
d. June 21, 1970 m. Lulu Hartmann (Cobb)
February 1914

Alva Elberta Spellman (Hartman) b. August 15, 1915
d. March 6, 2010 m. Clyde Dennis Spellman
December 28, 1934 b. January 1, 1914 d. January
26, 1985

Dennis Clyde Spellmann b. February 19, 1936 d.
August 30, 2000 m. Carol Sue Spellmann
(Spreckelmeyer) b. June 26, 1936

Sheryl Kay Spellmann (Guffey) b. October 29, 1957 m.
John Robert Guffey b. October 14, 1953

Ryan Vance Guffey b. January 6, 1981 m. Laura
(Feuerbacher) Guffey dau. Adalyn Kay Guffey b.
June 8, 2011, Son Vance Robert Guffey b. Aug 29.
2013

Daniel Dennis Guffey b. August 27, 1984 m. Tara
Guffey (Gresco), Son Connor Thomas Guffey b.
August 27, 2014, Son William Daniel Guffey b.
March 22, 2017

Zadock Woods and Minerva Woods (Cottle)

*Norman Woods b. October 3, 1805 at Woods Fort d.
December 16, 1843 in Perote Prison, Mexico m.
Jane Boyd Wells 1831

Ardelia Woods (Glimp) b. January 3, 1833 m. Tom
Glimp 1852
Sarah Caroline Spellmann (Glimp) b. February 23,
1856 d. April 15, 1943 m. **Ernst Christian
Spellmann** June 30, 1878 b. 1835 d. 1866

**Papa Ernst and Mama
Caroline   Spellmann
with children Frank,
Anna,   Christian,
Uhland,   Paul,
Bertha,   and   Lizzie
(1893)** Picture from
Woods-Cottle-Harrell
Family Web Site (2011)

**Ernst Christian and Nora
Wedding (October 9, 1909)**
Picture owned by Laurence
Spellman   posted   on
Woods-Cottle-Harrell Family
Web Site (2000)

Clyde Dennis Spellman m.
Alva Spellman (Hartman)

Ernst Christian Spellmann b. January 9, 1883 d. 1897
and Nora Lee Spellmann (Smith) b. July 13, 1883
d. 1971

Dennis Clyde Spellmann
m. Carol Sue Spellmann
(Spreckelmeyer)
**Sheryl Kay Spellmann
(Guffey)
Ryan Vance Guffey**
m. Laura Guffey
(Feuerbacher) dau. Adalyn
Kay Guffey, Vance Guffey
Daniel Dennis Guffey
m. Tara Guffey (Gresco)
Connor Guffey, William
Guffey

*The Spellman (n) family added and dropped the "n," perhaps to show a more or less German spelling before and after World War II.

Founders of Troy, Missouri

Deacon Joseph Cottle and **Zadock Woods** received the first two grants recorded in the administrative books of the St. Charles District of Upper Louisiana for American settlers in 1801. The official Spanish record for Zadock's Spanish Land Grant is found in the "Spanish French Registre de Arpentage Rive Gauche du Missouri B." The grants were 60 miles northwest of St. Louis on the Cuivre River. Joseph built the first horse-mill in the St. Charles District.

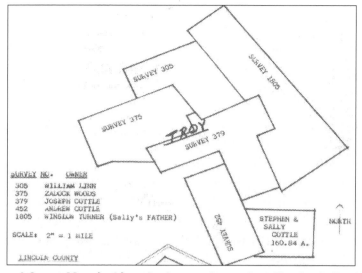

Land Grant Map in Lincoln County Image from The Cottle Family Genealogy supplement xi by James B. Schwabe (1981)

Major Christopher Clark from Kentucky built a home in the area in 1801, as did the Cottles and Woods. The Sac and Fox Indians numbered about the same population as the City of St. Louis. Later, in Cuivre Township, Deacon Joseph Cottle, Andrew Cottle, Issac Cottle, Jacob Cottle, Zadock Woods, and Sylvanus Cottle

were presented land grants. All settlers were required to swear their allegiance to the Spanish crown and the Catholic faith; however, there was no requirement to actually convert to Catholicism. Captain Warren Cottle led a group of 20 men against Indian depredations in the Cuivre settlement in 1804. The St. Charles County Historical Archives reveal the first tax records against the Cottle family in Lincoln County, was dated in 1805.

Life was hard in this territory. "The Cottles and Woods provisions became so scarce that after awhile nothing was left but musty meal." Carter, *Territorial Papers of the United States*," Vol. XIV, 1804-1814. A stockade was built to surround the 12 cabins of the frontier families. Joseph Cottle and Zadock Woods built Woods Fort (an almost square stockade) in present-day Troy to enclose the spring, cabins, Woods Tavern & Inn, and the Universalist church where Joseph served as Deacon. Woods Fort served as a shelter during the War of 1812 against the British and Indians under the leadership of Chief Black Hawk.

In the Fort Osage Journals and Letters of George Sibley (Founder of Lindenwood University), there is an entry dated Thursday, January 31, 1811 concerning Issac Cottle.

> "Morning cloudy and cool. Mr. Isaac Cottle started this morning for the Settlements on the Quiver in company with three other men. Sent my public dispatches by Mr. Cottle under cover to General Clark, securely wrapped in Buckskin; also a Small packet to Mr. Comegys enclosing a Letter to him and one for J. Gales Jr., Washington City for him to forward by mail. Mr. Cottle says he will deliver these packets as soon as possible and take special care of them while in his hands."

Jeffery Smith, *Seeking a Newer World: The Fort Osage Journals and Letters of George Sibley 1808-1811* (St. Charles, Missouri: Lindenwood University Press).

Zadock Woods Muster Roll 1812
Image from *The Cottle Family Genealogy* by James B. Schwabe (1977)

The pioneers were aided by Lieut. Zachary Taylor—later General and the 12th President of the United States—in 1813. The Rangers under Captain Daniel Boone and Captain Nathan Boone, as well as Captain James Calloway, were also in command at Woods Fort. Zadock, along with his father-in law, Joseph, and brother-in-law, Leander F. T. Cottle, are credited with founding Troy in 1819. The Cottle and Woods family deeded Woods Fort and the spring to the public in September of 1819.

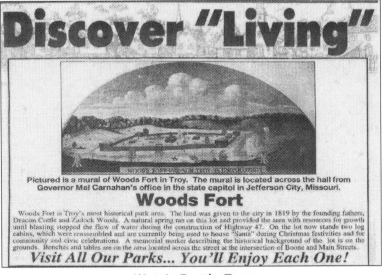

Discover "Living"

Pictured is a mural of Woods Fort in Troy. The mural is located across the hall from Governor Mel Carnahan's office in the state capitol in Jefferson City, Missouri.

Woods Fort

Woods Fort is Troy's most historical park area. The land was given to the city in 1819 by the founding fathers, Deacon Cottle and Zadock Woods. A natural spring ran on this lot and provided the area with resources for growth until blasting stopped the flow of water during the construction of Highway 47. On the lot now stands two log cabins, which were reassembled and are currently being used to house "Santa" during Christmas festivities and for community and civic celebrations. A memorial marker describing the historical background of the lot is on the grounds. Benches and tables are on the area located across the street at the intersection of Boone and Main Streets.

Visit All Our Parks... You'll Enjoy Each One!

Woods Fort in Troy
Picture from a Troy newspaper advertisement (2007)

The location of the fort began near the northeast corner of the current Baptist Church of Troy, Lot 166; thence up the road (Main Street) north about 70 yards; thence west some 40 yards; then to the south and east, enclosing the Spring and the Woods and Cottle homes.

Zadock Woods went to Kentucky to fight Indians under Andrew Jackson and then went to New Orleans. After the War of 1812, Zadock lost most of his family fortune when he invested, with Moses and Stephen Austin, in a mining venture in Potosi, Missouri. Zadock, Minerva, and five of their six children, moved to Texas and erected another fort for the new colony similar to the one built in Troy, Missouri.

James Addison Darby Home. What was left of Woods Fort Ca 1900, Fayette County. On the porch: James W. Moore and Middie Darby Moore on left. Lucius Campbell in chair on far right. In front of fence: Uncle John Darby. Seated: Aunt Carie holding Darby Moore Prastik. Sue Moore Elhers standing next to Aunt Carie. Charlie the horse on far left.

Woods Fort in Texas
Image from The Cottle-Woods-Harrell family web site (2011)

In 1812, Spain opened her Texas province for colonization. Zadock and his sons applied for citizenship and land grants through a colonizer, Stephen F. Austin. The Woods were among the first families of "The Old Three Hundred." This is according to L.U., Spellmann in *A Record of the Spellmann Family 1878-1964* (July 28, 1964). ("The Old Three Hundred" were the land grant recipients in Austin's first colony in Texas in 1824.) Zadock and his sons fought in many battles against the Mexican army, including the battle at San Jacinto on April 21, 1836. Zadock died in the Dawson Massacre, near San Antonio on September 18, 1842—his 69th birthday. A rock tomb monument has been erected on Monument Hill overlooking LaGrange, Texas honoring the fallen comrades of this battle.

Monument over Heroes Tomb
Picture by: Loma Neil Laman Ranne (2000)

Founders of Old Monroe

Ira, his cousin Almond, and Col. Nathaniel Simonds moved north to settle the area on the Cuivre River in 1801. In 1802, they furnished the land and established the town of Old Monroe. Martin and James Woods and their parents, Jonathan and Keziah Woods, as well as Joseph Cottle, also settled in Old Monroe.

In 1804, Hannah Cottle, widow of Martial Cottle, married Col. Nathaniel Simonds. In 1818, Ira was elected as Representative from St. Charles County to the last territorial general assembly and was commissioner for laying out the roads in Monroe Township. Ira was instrumental in the formation of Lincoln County, serving as a court justice from 1821 until 1824 at the three county seats at Old Monroe, Alexander, and Troy. "In 1821 Ira was listed as owner of 1,000 acres of choice land in the area." Houck's History of Missouri, 1908 Vol. III, p 8). Ira had 2,415.71 acres when he died at Old Monroe in 1842.

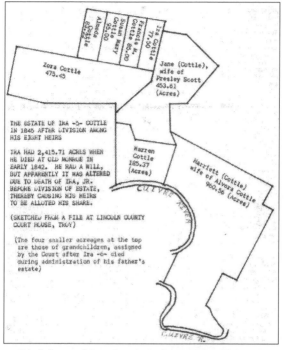

Division of Ira Cottle's Property (1845)
Image from The Cottle Genealogy by James B. Schwabe (1981)

Mr. Ira Cottle, of St. Charles County, once had a difficulty with Hon. Benjamin Emmons, Sr., about a calf, each claiming it as his property. They finally concluded to try Solomon on the calf, and let it decide which cow was its mother. So it was turned into a lot with two cows, and at first it ran to the one owned by Cottle. "Aha!" he exclaimed, greatly elated, "I told you it was my calf-see how it runs to its mother." But about this time the calf discovered its mistake and ran to the other cow, and remained with her. "Confound the calf," said Cottle, "it don't know its own mother." But it had decided against him, and according to the terms of the agreement he was bound to submit, which he did with as good grace as he could command. *History of St. Charles County p. 124.*

Hannah (Bailey) Cottle married Col. Nathaniel Simonds, founder of Old Monroe, opened a hotel in St. Charles where Hannah oversaw the cooking for the Lewis and Clark Expedition while they were in town (1804).

Cottle County, Texas was named to honor **George Washington Cottle**, who died while helping defend the Alamo. His ancestors were: Jonathan, Sylvanus, John, and Edward Cottle. George Washington Cottle was killed during the massacre of the defenders of the Alamo on March 6, 1836.

Josephine Owaissa Cottle, born April 5, 1922, is better known as **Gale Storm** of the 1952-55 television series *My Little Margie.* Josephine was a TV and nightclub entertainer. She has four stars on the Hollywood Walk of Fame for her contributions to radio, music, television, and motion pictures. Josephine died on June 27, 2009.

Walter Lester Cottle, donated land to Santa Clara County and the State of California worth many millions of dollars, after his death at age 88. His grandfather, Martial Cottle gave the land to his daughter, Ethel Cottle Lester, who passed it on to her children, Walter Cottle Lester and his late sister, Edith. The donation helped Lester avoid the vast majority of a more than $100 million estate tax bill associated with the death of this sister. The 150 year Cottle legacy can be seen in the heart of Silicon Valley and will be preserved forever with Martial Cottle Park, picnic areas, a visitor's center and land for farming.

Cottle Burying Ground

Father Pezold, on a bright summer day in 1972, took my father Dennis Spellmann and myself to see Tate Drieswerd. He was the farmer on Wies Road that owned the property belonging to the original Cottle family and the Cottle Cemetery. I saw several of the Cottle tombstones around the foundation of his basement. In June of 1977, James and Opal Hannah visited Cottleville, Missouri, with the intention of locating the old Cottle Burying Ground Cemetery, but found none. They then went to Oak Grove Cemetery and took data from the Cottle gravestones. "There we visited the gravestone honoring Captain Warren Cottle, sponsored by the D.A.R. Perhaps the word gravestone is misleading, for his remains are not there, but presumably are on the farm at the site of the old "Cottle Cemetery." (James Hannah.) Unfortunately, Mr. Drieswerd sold the property never disclosing the cemetery and development projects began as Cottleville moved from being a village to a city around 1992. Tate Drieswerd was the son of John Drieswerd and a relative of Frank Martin.

Page 6A Friday, June 9, 1995—JOURNAL

Cemetery improperly deeded, city claims

By Dawn Adams Huffman
Correspondent

Cottleville is disputing the legality of a family cemetery established east of the Dardenne Farms subdivision along Hwy. N.

The problem can be fixed easily enough -- if the owners of the cemetery cooperate with the city, City Attorney Charles Niedner said.

A few months ago, Terrance Piper buried his mother-in-law on his property, Niedner said.

At the time, the property was located in unincorporated St. Charles County. Since then, Cottleville has annexed the cemetery.

Both St. Charles County and Cottleville require that land designated as a private cemetery consist of at least 20 acres.

Piper owns more than 20 acres, but when he recorded a deed naming St. Charles County as trustee of the cemetery he only parceled off .85 acres, Niedner said. He said the deed fails to fulfill the 20-acre requirement.

So Cottleville asked Piper, through his attorney, Roland Moerschel, to file a deed restriction on the property that would designate 20 acres as a cemetery, Niedner said.

Even with such a deed restriction, the 20 acres could be used for agriculture, Niedner said. The restriction would prevent the subdividing and sale of the land for other uses, leaving a small, isolated plot for the private cemetery, he said.

There is no problem with establishing a cemetery on 20 acres in either the county or the city, Niedner said. But permitting cemeteries on smaller pieces of land would allow an undesirable proliferation of small burial plots, he said.

"The point of it (the law) really is to prevent every Tom, Dick or Harry from having hundreds and thousands of private cemeteries deeded to the county," Niedner said.

Niedner said Moerschel contended in a letter to him that the county zoning ordinance was void and unenforceable.

At its meeting June 1, the Board of Aldermen instructed Niedner to draw up a deed restriction and send it to Moerschel this week.

Moerschel said that only family members would be buried in the cemetery, and that the cemetery would never even come close to taking up 20 acres. He said he was still researching the matter, and would like to arrange a meeting with representatives of the city soon.

In the meantime, Niedner said he also would inform St. Charles County that the deed filed with the county doesn't meet the 20-acre requirement.

In St. Charles County and some other counties, deeds can be recorded over to the county without the county's assent, he said, so it can end up with deeds it doesn't even know about. Niedner said he wanted to alert the county to the problem with the Piper deed.

At the same time, Niedner said this particular cemetery is of concern to Cottleville because it is now within city limits.

Sheryl Kay Guffey

*The following is a letter written in 1933 describing what Kate Gregg found at the old "Cottle Burying Ground":

LINDENWOOD COLLEGE
FOUNDED IN 1827
ST. CHARLES, MISSOURI

DEPARTMENT OF ENGLISH

Feb.6, 1933

Dear Mrs. Adams:

"——Since I wrote you last I have been out to read the tombstones in the Cottle graveyard near Cottleville. The old vandal who now has possession of the place has stacked all the tombstones in a neat pile, and to read them I had to stand them up and lay them aside to get at the one underneath. Well, I made a copy of every gravestone in the pile, and sent you a carbon copy for your own records, for chances are that the old rascal who now owns the place will entirely destroy them before long. The gravestone of Dr. Warren Cottle has already disappeared, all but a few fragments, just enough to see that it was his.

Yours most cordially,
Kate L. Gregg

List of graves at the Cottle Burying Ground

Warren Cottle
Native of Vermont
(Original stone is at the Cottleville City Hall)

In Memory of
Marshall Cottle
Wife of Hannah Bailey Cottle
Died September 4, 1801
Aged 22 Yr

Marcial
Son of M. (Marshall) & Hannah Cottle
Grandson of Warren Cottle

Lorenzo Cottle
Consecrated in Memory of Lorenzo Cottle
born Sept.11,1811 died Sept 26, 1892
(Stone moved from Cottle Burying Ground to Oak
Grove Cemetery)

SALOME
Wife of Warren Cottle
Died Oct. 3, 1847 Aged 65 Yrs. 10 Mo. 18 Da.
Native of Woodstock, Vermont

Sarah Ann Green
Wife of Lorenzo Cottle
Died
May 12, 1862
Aged
33 Yrs. 5 Mo. 19 Da.

VIOLETTA
Wife of Lorenzo Cottle
Died Jan.5, 1853
Aged 34 Yrs. 8 Mo. 11 Da.

Mary P.
Daughter of L. and V. Cottle
Died Dec. 17, 1851

Henry B.
Son of L. & S.A. Cottle
Died Sept. 10, 1859
Aged 1 Yr. 1 Mo. 24 Da.
"A sweet little boy"
Henry F.
Son of Ora & E. Cottle
Died Dec. 10, 1851
Aged 11 Mo. 24 Da.

Infant Dau.
Died Aug. 30, 1865

HELENA
Wife of Frederick Busch
Born Sept. 8, 1806
Died July 16, 1852

Albert Busch
Geb. 28 April 1819
Gest. 22 Jan. 1872

Allen Farnsworth
Died April 26, 1862
Aged 62 Yr. 11 Mo. 28 Da.

Abigail
Wife of A. Farnsworth
Died Sept.4, 1827
Aged 28 Yr. 11 Mo.28 Da.
Emily
Dau. of A. & A. Farnsworth
Died Jan. 11, 1825
Aged 2 Yr. 5 Mo. 7 Da.

Biel Farnsworth
Native of New Hampshire
Died April 2, 1847
Aged 74 Yr. 3 Mo. 23 Da.

Erected in Memory of
Mrs. Missouri Ann Fowler
Dau. of Lorenzo Cottle & Sarah Ann, his wife
Born April 20, A.D., 1855
and departed this life July 18, A.D., 1875
"Erected to her by her father and brother"

Izetta Yarnell
Dau. of T. Foreman
Born November 8, 1873
Died September 29, 1903
Aged 29 Yr. 10 Mo. 21 Da.
"I have lost my darling wife
She has bid us all adieu
She has gone to lie in heaven
And her person is lost to view
Oh, that dear one how l
we loved her
Oh, how hard it is to give
her up
But an Angel came down for her
And removed her from our flock"

Cottle Grave Stones at Oak Grove Cemetery in St. Charles, Missouri

Capt. Warren Cottle d. 1811

Violetta Killam Cottle (McClay) d. January 5, 1853

Sarah M. Cottle d. May, 31, 1891

Lorenzo Cottle d. September 26, 1892

Edward Francis Cottle d. April 4, 1915

Laura Elizabeth Cottle (White) d. June, 14, 1916

Oliver Thomas Cottle d. 1935

J. Othello Cottle d. 1949 Masonic Emblem Past Master, Constitution Lodge 426 Ohio F and A.M.

Bertha Albert Cottle d. Feb. 1, 1974

Juanita Cottle (Stephens) d. Feb. 15, 1980

Dr. Eugene Cottle d. September, 7, 1988

Dr. Dennis C. Spellmann d. August 30, 2006

Cottle Grave Stones at Mount Zion Cemetery in O'Fallon, Missouri

Henry Warren Cottle b. September 1, 1876 d. November 7, 1891

Walter Britton Cottle b. January 6, 1879 d. November 7, 1891

Alice Virginia Cottle b. January 8, 1889 d. February 1, 1896

Alice Virginia Cottle (Stephenson) b. December 13, 1855 d. April 3, 1913

Samuel Warren Cottle b. October 3, 1846 d. June 15, 1921

Bessie Lee Cottle b. January 17, 1884 d. December 23, 1948

Cottle Grave Stones at Troy, Missouri

Alzinza Cottle d. May 22, 1830

Almond Cottle d. January 14, 1835

Andrew Cottle d. November 21, 1841

Ardelia Cottle d. March 5, 1843
Rebecca Cottle d. October 5, 1845
Drucilla Cottle d. December 11, 1846
Sherman Cottle d. June, 25, 1854
Andrew Cottle d. July, 10, 1848
Maggie Cottle d. September 6, 1898
E.D.C. Cottle d. April 21, 1908
Stephen Cottle d. March 24, 1910
William Sherman Cottle d. December 9, 1918
Patty Cottle d. August 15, 1929
Mary Frances Cottle d. March 5, 1930
Sarah B. Cottle d. April 5, 1930
Ceclia Carol Cottle d. May 18, 1941
William W. Cottle d. February 19, 1945
William M. Cottle d. March 6, 1946
Lucy Cottle (Penn) d. June 12, 1947
William A. Cottle d. September 18, 1967

Gravestones at Highland Prairie Cemetery – Old Monroe

Mary Cottle b. October 7, 1843 d. January 13, 1914

L. B. Cottle b. April 17, 1838 d. June 28, 1916

GRAVESTONES AT WOLF

Aarons, Mary b. 1876 d. 1909

Aarons, Mary K. b. Jun. 18, 1876 d. Oct. 3, 1909

Aarons, Tom b. 1874 d. 1941

Arras, Charles b. Feb. 11, 1866 d. Oct. 29, 1936

Arras, Elizabeth b. 1845 d. Feb. 7, 1917

Arras, Ida May b. 1877 d. 1961

Arras, John b. May 25, 1833 d. Dec. 5, 1924

Arras, John Adam b. May 7, 1795 d. Feb. 24, 1852

Arras, Mary E. b. Oct. 16, 1868 d. Aug. 4, 1964

Berthold, Adam b. Oct. 1, 1873 d. Oct. 1, 1873

Berthold, Adam b. Nov. 13, 1887 d. Nov. 15, 1887

Berthold, Anna b. Jul. 11, 1839 d. Nov. 17, 1875

Berthold, Anna M. b. Sep. 5, 1872 d. Feb. 26, 1873

Berthold, Christine b. Nov. 13, 1887 d. Nov. 15, 1887

Berthold, Conrad b. Oct. 3, 1871 d. Oct. 8, 1871

Berthold, Conrad b. Aug. 6, 1820 d. Aug. 5, 1866

Berthold, Conrad b. Mar. 21, 1851 d. Oct. 30, 1902

Berthold, Gertrude b. Aug. 20, 1881 d. Aug. 20, 1881

Berthold, Infant Child b. unknown d. unknown

Berthold, Infant Child b. unknown d. unknown

Berthold, Infant Son b. Nov. 2, 1885 d. Nov. 2, 1885

Berthold, John b. Aug. 20, 1881 d. Aug. 20, 1881

Berthold, John M. b. Oct. 28, 1858 d. ???. 27, 1907

Berthold, Katherina *Gutermuth* b. Sep. 1, 1851 d. Mar. 26, 1928

Berthold, Louisa b. Aug. 13, 1859 d. Mar. 20, 1916

Croft, Elisabeth b. unknown d. unknown

Croft, Thomas b. unknown d. unknown

Fetch, Adam A. b. Jan. 11, 1874 d. Apr. 13

Fetch, Cornelia b. Mar. 21, 1871 d. Feb. 26, 1873

Fetch, Elisabeth A. b. May 26, 1877 d. Oct. 12, 1877

Fetch, John W. b. Oct. 14, 1872 d. Mar. 3, 1873

Fisher, Conrad Fred b. Oct. 18, 1879 d. Jul. 13, 1901

Fisher, Maria Katherine *Rose* b. 1839 d. Mar. 8, 1898

Fisher, Phillip b. Dec., 1837 d. Nov. 29, 1905

Gutermuth, Adam August b. Feb. 24, 1862 d. 1862

Gutermuth, Infant b. Aug. 1, 1884 d. Jul. 29, 1885

Gutermuth, Johann B b. Sep. 21, 1812 d. Jun. 29, 1969

Hahn, John A. b. Sep. 9, 1836 d. Jan. 12, 1876

GRAVESTONES AT PITMAN CEMETERY

Branson, John Franklin b. 1889 d. Jan. 12, 1921

Campbell, Eliza F. b. 1818 d. 1910

Castlio, Eleanor *Harrison* b. unknown d. 1811

Dorsey, Lloyd b. Oct. 6, 1806 d. May 29, 1876

Glanville, Annie *Pitman* b. Nov. 26, 1835 d. Mar. 5, 1856

Glanville, William Stephen b. 1823 d. Jan. 13, 1864

Pitman, Caroline Hickman b. Oct. 1, 1832 d. Dec. 19, 1836

Pitman, David Baker b. May 5, 1843 d. Feb. 18, 1845

Pitman, David Kyle b. Dec. 2, 1805 d. Apr. 13, 1891

Pitman, Eliza Hamilton *Baker* b. May 25, 1813 d. Mar. 19, 1887

Pitman, Maj John b. Mar. 14, 1753 d. Jan. 1, 1839

Sanford, Angus C b. Jun. 23, 1853 d. Jun. 30, 1854

Sanford, Annie E b. Mar. 17, 1858 d. Aug. 12, 1858

Sanford, Elizabeth *Tidball* b. 1805 d. Jan. 1, 1872

Sanford, James Tidball b. Jan., 1828 d. Dec. 31, 1868

Sanford, Lucy H. b. 1827 d. 1920

Weinreben, Agenes b. unknown d. Jan. 26, 1865

Weinreben, Friedrich b. unknown d. Sep., 1874

Population of Cottleville - Through the Years

1817	735
1819	621
1846	500
1867	340
1880	225
1964	150
1970	230
1980	184
1990	2,936
2000	1928
2003	2,059
2006	2,596
2009	3,227
2010	3,075
2015	4,723
2016	3,836

Square miles 4.5 - 67.5% growth since the 2010 census